THE WISDOM
OF THE SOUL

PROFOUND INSIGHTS
FROM THE LIFE BETWEEN LIVES

IAN LAWTON

WITH RESEARCH ASSISTANCE
FROM ANDY TOMLINSON

First published in 2007 by Rational Spirituality Press, PO Box 5743, Southend-on-Sea, SS1 9AE, UK.

All enquiries to be directed to *www.rspress.org*

A CIP catalogue record for this title is available from the British Library.

ISBN 978-0-9549176-1-6
ISBN 0-9549176-1-8

Cover design by Ian Lawton.
Cover image by Jason Waskey.
www.jasonwaskey.com

Author photograph by James Franklin.
www.jamesfranklin.com

Printed and bound by Hobbs the Printers, Southampton, England.

Ian Lawton was born in 1959. In his mid-thirties he became a full-time writer-researcher specializing in ancient history, esoterica and spiritual philosophy. His first two books, *Giza: The Truth* (1999) and *Genesis Unveiled* (2003), were published by Virgin and have sold over 30,000 copies worldwide. In his third, *The Book of the Soul* (2004), he developed the idea of 'Rational Spirituality', in addition to establishing himself as one of the world's leading authorities on the interlife. For further information see *www.ianlawton.com*.

Andy Tomlinson graduated in psychology and is a UKCP registered psychotherapist. He is the Director of Training for the Past Life Regression Academy, and a founder member of the European Academy of Regression Therapy. He has written two books, *Healing the Eternal Soul* (2006) and *Exploring the Eternal Soul* (2007). Andy trains and lectures internationally on past lives and the interlife. For further information, and a list of past and between-life therapists, see *www.regressionacademy.com*.

CONTENTS

PREFACE   1

INTRODUCTION   3

Laying the foundations; the history of interlife research; the interlife experience; the reliability of interlife material; moving into the universal; the sources; the selection and presentation of transcript material.

1. UNUSUAL SOUL BEHAVIOR   17

Trapped energies, fragments and imprints; attachment of trapped energies; soul fragmentation; multiple incarnations; walk-ins; shared soul memories and projections; carrying over body traumas and physical characteristics; death-points and suicides; demonic beings.

2. SOUL DEVELOPMENT   51

The purpose of reincarnation; the Holographic Soul; human versus animal souls; soul birthing and the recycling of experience; reuniting with the Source; development during the reincarnation cycle; damaged, disoriented and impetuous souls; planes, levels and aspects; post-reincarnation development; experiencing other planets.

3. HUMANITY'S PAST AND FUTURE   90

The emergence of the human race; lost civilizations; the soul logistics of population increase; humanity's present problems and possible futures.

4. REALITY AND TIME   117

Creating our own reality; conscious co-creation; the nature of time and parallel dimensions.

5. CONCLUDING QUESTIONS   136

Possible conscious interference; variations in answers; subject feedback; summary; final messages; postscript.

APPENDIX I: RESEARCH APPROACH AND PROTOCOLS   148

The mechanics of interlife regression; the subjects; the questions; the sessions; processing the information.

APPENDIX II: THE RESEARCH QUESTIONS   157

GLOSSARY   161

SOURCE REFERENCES   167

BIBLIOGRAPHY   170

ACKNOWLEDGEMENTS

This book could not have come about without our subjects giving generously of their time to take part in a unique experiment, and to provide feedback afterwards. Andy and I would like to express our sincerest gratitude to all of them. Nor, clearly, is it possible to overestimate the crucial role played by the wise and experienced souls who made themselves available to act as sources of wisdom for our subjects to tap into.

Other people, too, have played a key part. Duncan Bain Smith kindly acted as the regressor when we wanted Andy to find out for himself what it was like to be a subject of the research program. Regression pioneers Edith Fiore and Hans TenDam both kindly took time out of their busy schedules to read the manuscript and provide useful feedback, as did my friends Ashley Bradbury, Mark Goodman, Philip Karhu, Yuri Leitch and David Southwell. And Ian Allen as always was hugely professional, thorough and helpful with the final editing. My heartfelt thanks go to all of them.

Last, but by no means least, my partner Liz Swanson not only acted as an initial sounding board for ideas – as well as providing some of her own – but also assisted me in the arduous task of transcribing over 100,000 words from the research tapes. In addition she put up with my long hours of preoccupied thinking and writing. So both I and this book owe her a very great deal.

PREFACE

The research in this book owes a huge amount to Andy Tomlinson. We first met in March 2004, because I was keen to experience past-life and interlife regression in order to incorporate my experiences into my last book, *The Book of the Soul*. As a psychology graduate and qualified psychotherapist, Andy has a broad combination of professional skills, including past-life hypnotherapy, and he has helped hundreds of people to overcome various psychological or physiological problems. But above all he is the UK's leading expert in spiritual regression because, having trained at the Michael Newton Institute in the US, he has enabled hundreds of clients to experience the incredible world that awaits us all after physical death – in our 'life between lives' or 'interlife'.

As we got to know each other better it became increasingly clear that we shared a similar spiritual worldview. Furthermore Andy was not only a terrific colleague in helping to spread the word about 'Rational Spirituality', but he also provided personal help and support when it was most needed. All this despite being heavily tied up in his own practice, and with his hugely important work in helping to establish and promote professional standards of regression training in Europe. Not only that, he was also engaged in writing his own first book, *Healing the Eternal Soul*, which is a highly readable yet professional contribution to the understanding of regression therapy.

Our collaborative research efforts sprang from a phone call in November 2005, when Andy asked if I would like to write a new book with him. Because in my last book I had collated, compared and analyzed the research published by a number of pioneering interlife therapists, we initially discussed how I could help him build on that research by sifting through and analyzing the several hundred case files he had accumulated. But it was towards the end of that initial phone call that an idea suddenly sprang into my head.

The interlife experience tends, broadly speaking, to be a *personal* one. But I was aware that several of the pioneers had managed to direct some subjects to answer a few rather more *universal* questions. So what if we could really push the boundaries by developing a structured set of questions about everything from trapped spirits to demonic beings, from the purpose of incarnation to life on other planets, from legends of Atlantis to the future of humanity, and from multiple realities to the true

1

nature of time? What if we then put them to, say, ten of Andy's best subjects? And what if their answers showed the high degree of consistency that has characterized so much interlife research to date? Andy liked the idea, and our universal research program was born.

We had originally intended to publish both our personal and universal research in one book. But as time wore on it became clear that the subject matter of each part would be somewhat different, would need to be presented somewhat differently, and above all might appeal to somewhat different audiences. So eventually, and after much deliberation, we took the decision to separate the two – and for Andy to take responsibility for one book, and myself the other. In this way we would be playing to our respective strengths.

Finally, this research is potentially only the starting point for a substantially new approach to uncovering profound spiritual insights. So Andy and I would be delighted if it inspires other properly qualified regression professionals to follow it up using similar methods and protocols to those described in detail in Appendix I.

Ian Lawton
February 2007

INTRODUCTION

Laying the Foundations

Most people are familiar with the idea of past-life regression. Normally although not exclusively achieved by entering a mild state of hypnotic trance, it allows vivid memories of lives gone by to resurface into consciousness, often with amazing clarity.

Of course skeptics dismiss all this as nonsense. They insist that past-life memories prove nothing but the ability of human imagination to construct a plausible story from a variety of information acquired by perfectly normal means over the course of their current life. And there can be little doubt that many past-life memories probably contain some elements of factual inaccuracy because of conscious influence. But to leave the analysis there, as most skeptics do, is to fall way short of properly investigating a phenomenon that is far too complex to be so lightly dismissed.

In fact there are several reasons to take past-life memories seriously. First, a considerable number of well-investigated cases are now on record in which subjects have recalled information that is not only subsequently verified, but also so obscure that it stretches credulity to its limits to suggest that they must somehow have obtained it via perfectly normal means. Nor, once all the circumstances and context of such cases are properly understood, is it remotely plausible to suggest that they all involved deliberate deception, which is the only other normal explanation that could hold water.

Second, although skeptics might suggest that most past-life therapists are unprofessional quacks who believe in reincarnation anyway, nothing could be further from the truth – at least as far as the early pioneers were concerned. Trailblazers such as Britons Alexander Cannon, Denys Kelsey and Roger Woolger, Americans Morris Netherton, Edith Fiore, Helen Wambach and Brian Weiss, Canadian Joel Whitton, Australian Peter Ramster and Dutchman Hans TenDam came to the fore in the fifties, sixties and seventies, and all were professionally trained psychologists and psychiatrists. Moreover nearly all of them describe how, whatever their background, they had developed an atheist or at least agnostic attitude while studying psychology at university. So even though they had all been trained to use conventional hypnotherapy to regress subjects back into their childhoods, most of them were initially skeptical when they either experimented with, or merely stumbled upon, regression into what appeared to be past lives. But many of them then found that some subjects, who might have failed to respond to conventional therapies over many years, made dramatic improvements after only a few sessions. Admittedly they all tend to stress that such therapeutic success does not rely on either therapist or subject believing in reincarnation. Nevertheless the majority came to the conclusion that this was no mere placebo, and that reincarnation is a reality.

Third, it is often reported that people only remember past lives in which they were a famous historic figure, and therefore the process is primarily fueled not only by imagination but also ego. But again this is a complete fallacy. Most past-life recall, certainly during controlled regression, involves lives that are 'nasty, brutish and short' – which matches the cultural conditions that have prevailed in our world for most of human history.

But it is not just past-life regression that should make us take the idea of reincarnation seriously. Another key area of complementary research involves children who spontaneously remember past lives, pioneered since the early sixties by Ian Stevenson and other members of the psychology department at the University of Virginia. They have professionally investigated and documented more than a thousand cases in which subjects again come up with subsequently verified information that is so obscure it could not have been obtained by normal means. They have also developed scientific protocols that are deliberately designed to root out the only other normal explanation, which is again deliberate fraud or collusion.

This is necessarily an extremely short summary of evidence that I present in far more detail in *The Book of the Soul*, because the main focus of this book is not on proof of past lives and reincarnation. But hopefully it provides an important foundation, showing why we should take this subject seriously.

Before we continue there is one other crucial issue to be considered. Some of Stevenson's cases also involve children with unusual birthmarks or other defects that have been shown, by postmortem reports and so on, to correspond exactly to the wounds that killed their previous personality – of whose life other obscure details have again been provided and verified. This evidence, among other things, is a most potent argument that at least some past-life memories derive from the individual soul's reincarnatory experience, and not from tapping into some sort of universal memory or collective unconscious. Although we will return to this in far more detail in due course, this is a crucial factor that should be borne in mind by anyone who is drawn to the view that the reincarnation cycle – indeed even the whole notion of soul individuality – is illusory.

The History of Interlife Research

If the pioneering therapists were surprised by the results of their research into past lives, imagine the added surprise when, in the mid-seventies, several of them independently discovered that their subjects could recall details of their time *between lives* as well. All of a sudden, ordinary people with no particular religious or spiritual background began to deliver profound insights into the 'interlife' experience. Even more impressive was that their revelations proved to be highly consistent.

Whitton's experience was typical of a number of his successors in that he gave an imprecise command to a subject with whom he had already undertaken a great deal of past-life work. During one of these sessions he instructed her to go back to the 'life' – rather than 'incarnation' – before the one she had just been regressed into, and was amazed to find her describing herself as 'in the sky... waiting to be born... watching my mother'. He would go on to make a huge contribution to our understanding of the interlife experience by deliberately investigating the phenomenon with a number of his more responsive subjects, publishing his research in his 1986 collaboration with Joe Fisher, *Life Between Life*.

By contrast Wambach deliberately instigated a research program in which she regressed volunteers in groups. Having already achieved great success in garnering the first real statistical data about past lives using this method, she decided to try to take 750 of her volunteers back to the time before they were born into this life. She asked about whether they chose to return, whether anyone helped them in their decision, and how they felt about coming back. Again her results, published in 1979 in *Life Before Life*, were impressive.

Around the same time Fiore was beginning to amass a considerable amount of interlife material, but unfortunately a variety of tragic circumstances led to her mislaying all her relevant case notes and drafts before she could publish it. Despite this a few strands can be found in her first two books, *You Have Been Here Before* and *The Unquiet Dead*, published in 1978 and 1988 respectively. Meanwhile, although Ramster too was not concentrating primarily on investigating the interlife, he was simultaneously making some important discoveries that were incorporated into *The Truth About Reincarnation* and *The Search for Lives Past*, published in 1980 and 1990 respectively.

Over the next decade or so three more interlife pioneers came to the fore, all in America. Dolores Cannon stumbled upon it again by accident when a subject died in a past life and then began describing how they were 'floating above their body', and her further research was published in 1993 in *Between Death and Life*. Meanwhile, although Shakuntala Modi's research is arguably somewhat biased by her Christian outlook and concentration on demonic possession – something most of the other pioneers dismiss – her 1997 book *Remarkable Healings* contains some highly consistent summaries of her findings about the interlife.

Finally we come to Michael Newton, who has been more successful than any other pioneer in bringing interlife research into the public consciousness. Typically he too was skeptical about past-life regression when he set up his hypnotherapy practice in the mid fifties. But after some years he began to appreciate its capabilities when a subject, directed to go to the source of a pain in his right side, described being stabbed as a soldier in World War One – and his persistent pain was immediately and permanently relieved. Not long after this he also stumbled upon the interlife by accident when issuing an imprecise command to another subject who was particularly receptive to entering deeper states of hypnotic trance. From that point on he concentrated most of his efforts on investigating the phenomenon as thoroughly as he could, publishing his findings in *Journey of Souls* and *Destiny of Souls* in 1994 and 2000 respectively, before going on to set up his own institute dealing in training and other aspects of what he refers to as 'spiritual regression'.

The Interlife Experience

The key aspect of this pioneering interlife research is the consistency of the underlying elements of the experience reported by subjects, and in *The Book of the Soul* I collated and analyzed all the pioneers' research in considerable detail to demonstrate this consistency. However a number of new ideas have emerged from the personal interlife research Andy and I have conducted together more recently, which is presented in his second book *Exploring the Eternal Soul*. The following summaries of the five main elements of the interlife experience include these new ideas.

Transition and Healing

During this phase we shed the heavier and denser emotions and energies associated with the physical plane so that our soul energy gradually becomes lighter and less dense. Our recent research has found that interlife regression subjects often refer to 'moving through or shedding layers', and we have coined the term 'delayering' to describe this process. It is inextricably linked with emotional healing, and less experienced souls are usually assisted with this, whether they are aware of it or not, while more traumatized souls require more intense initial healing. It also represents *the* essential process by which we raise our vibration level sufficiently to return to our true home in the 'light realms' – because without it we simply cannot operate at these higher frequencies.

Research conducted initially by Newton and confirmed by us has indicated that we usually make a deliberate decision about how much of our soul energy to take into incarnation, thereby leaving some of it behind in the light realms. We might regard this as our 'higher' or 'soul self'. So an additional aspect of our transition is that at some point we will need to reunite with the energy we left behind, at which point we receive another dramatic infusion of soul energy and awareness.

Past-Life Review

Either as part of our initial healing, or not long afterwards, we will usually participate in some kind of review of the life just passed. We may do this alone; we may be aided by our spirit guide, who is a more experienced soul available to help us both in incarnation and during the interlife; or we may be aided by our elders, a group of still-wiser souls who help us to plot a path through our successions of lives. Some subjects describe such reviews as taking place in a 'library' environment in which the books in front of them 'come alive' like a film. Others even suggest that they can 'enter' the film to replay various events, or even to 'role-play' them by doing things differently and seeing what happens. And some report that they can place themselves in the shoes of others, to see exactly what effect their actions had on them.

Above all, however, during such reviews the only judgment comes, if at all, from *ourselves* – and not from the more experienced souls that might be assisting us. This is because our 'soul perspective' is totally unlike our human perceptions, and cannot include self-deception or excuses. All our actions and, even more important, our intentions are laid bare. And it is up to us, aided by our spirit guides and elders, to cope with our reaction to them.

Soul Group Learning

All of us have a group of soul mates with whom we work closely in varied relationships over many lives, and our reunion with them is always a profoundly moving experience. But, as I emphasized in *The Book of the Soul*, the primary aim of all souls is to learn, experience and grow. So our time with our soul group is often characterized by discussions about lives we have shared, how we reacted to each other, what we handled well and what we could have handled better. In this context the ability to replay and role-play events once more comes to the fore. Moreover we sporadically move to a different soul group to work on new lessons.

But what do we really mean by 'learning'? It is apparent that in the first instance we all have to work on what we now refer to as 'emotional lessons', and to see both sides of every emotional coin. So we all need to experience not only all of the less attractive emotions such as loss, guilt, failure, shame, remorse, selfishness, sorrow, humiliation, jealousy, anger, hatred and revenge, but also the counterbalancing emotions such as patience, altruism, openness, understanding, forgiveness, acceptance and, ultimately and most powerfully, love – in all its guises. But in order to experience and understand these fully and properly, and to learn from them, we need to not only feel them *ourselves*, but also to feel what it is like to have them *directed at us* by others.

Such emotional learning can often be characterized by somewhat *repetitive* patterns of behavior, as we attempt to master particular emotions in a variety of life settings. However as souls gain in experience they start to move into more *progressive* patterns of behavior, which tend to be characterized by a more altruistic attitude. In particular, they start to develop the theme of what we now refer to as 'altruistic skills' – such as healing, teaching, guiding and so on – which they put into practice both in the physical and the light realms, often as part of a soul group who share the same skill set. In addition they increasingly choose to take on more 'altruistic lives', which tend to be primarily for other people's benefit and learning rather than their own. The most obvious example of this is when souls volunteer for short lives that end in childhood or even before birth. Although such lives can sometimes be traumatic for the infants themselves, they tend to be far more aimed at challenging parents and other close relatives to learn to cope with the myriad emotions that surround such a tragic loss.

Next-Life Planning

At some point before our return we will usually engage in some sort of planning of our next life. At the very least this will involve an awareness of who our parents will be, where they live, their circumstances, and what sex we will be. But many subjects reveal that they receive a rather fuller preview, often describing it as akin to seeing a film that they can stop, rewind, fast-forward, and even enter to fully experience what is going on. We may even be given a preview of several different lives, and be asked to choose which one we think will be of most use to our learning and growth. And, as usual, our spirit guides and elders are on hand to provide assistance and advice. We may also spend some time discussing our plans with other members of our soul group who will be involved in that life, and even agreeing 'triggers' that will help us to recognize them when we meet.

Our planning is probably the most crucial aspect of the interlife experience, because it indicates that we have complete control over, and personal responsibility for, our lives. However in order to understand this properly we need to be clear that any life previews we glimpse represent major *probabilities* and lesser *possibilities* only. Our lives are not predetermined, and we have complete free will to depart from our 'plan'.

Returning

One key aspect of our return into incarnation is our decision about the level of soul energy to bring back. Although we may want to leave as much behind as possible to allow it to carry on with various aspects of learning and growth in the light realms, if we return to the physical with too little – especially if we face a difficult life – then we reduce our ability to see our plan through. Andy has also specifically built on Newton's research by establishing that we make additional decisions about what proportions of specific emotions we want to bring back to carry on working with, and even of past-life strengths that we may need to help us through difficult patches. Moreover, some of his subjects have indicated that this is achieved by what we now refer to as a 'relayering' process, in which they take on these heavier emotions as if putting on various layers of clothing.

The return is concluded by us finding ourselves in the womb, at anywhere from the point of conception to just before birth. The process of merging our soul energy with the new physical body is a gradual and sometimes difficult one, involving matching the individual pattern and frequency of our soul energy to that of the developing brain. Subjects also report that the stress of this process can be reduced by floating out of the body for short periods, and such activity may even carry on for some time after birth. However another aspect of our return is the gradual weakening of our connection to the light realms, and the gradual lowering of the 'veil of amnesia'. The general reason for this is twofold: first, if we knew all about our life plans in advance it would be like taking an exam with all the answers, and we would learn nothing; and second, if we remembered too much about the bliss of the light realms we would be constantly homesick and longing to return.

One of the major conclusions to emerge from the personal interlife research that Andy and I have conducted is the degree of *fluidity* of the experience. Although the elements described above provide a consistent, underlying thread, they are not all experienced by every subject during every interlife regression. Sometimes the emphasis may be more on review, or on planning, or on our soul-group theme. This does not necessarily mean that each of the elements is not experienced during the interlife *proper* at least to some degree. But it does mean that, when we are recalling the experience in human form, some things may be more important than others.

We should also recognize that, broadly speaking, each interlife experience between each pair of earthly lives is unique and different for each of us. However, subjects also report that the interlife proper represents an 'eternal now', in which not only elapsed but even sequential time becomes largely unimportant. So our recall of our time in the light realms under regression is only an approximation of the true, timeless experience – and it is deliberately framed in terms that our somewhat restricted human perceptions can understand.

The Reliability of Interlife Material

The consistency of the interlife experience reported by the pioneers' subjects did not emerge from just a few cases. Newton in particular reports that he built up a huge volume of case studies running not just into the hundreds but the thousands. Of course a skeptic might assume that this impressive consistency resulted from all the pioneers' subjects having specific belief systems or prior knowledge, or from the pioneers themselves sharing their information or engaging in undue 'subjective leading'. But close scrutiny suggests that the possibility of any of these factors playing a major role is negligible.

If we start with the subjects themselves, they were in most cases ordinary people who had at least originally come to the various pioneers for therapy. Indeed most of them emphasize that their subjects' prior belief systems varied enormously, covering the entire spectrum from atheism and agnosticism through all of the major religions, and above all that this seemed to make no difference whatsoever to the nature of the interlife experience. The only real exception to this may be Wambach's volunteers, many of whom probably had at least a prior belief in reincarnation.

As to subjects having prior knowledge of the interlife itself, this is highly unlikely to have occurred on any significant scale because most of the pioneers' books quoted above were nothing like bestsellers at the time. The possible exception to this is Newton, but his first publication did not come out until long after those of the other pioneers, and so could not have influenced their subjects.

Were the pioneers influenced by each other to any significant degree? Certainly in their books none of them mention any of the others, except that Modi does refer briefly to the work of Wambach and Whitton – but she was a relative latecomer anyway. Several of them do refer to the well-known and not unrelated work of Raymond Moody into near-death experiences and of Stevenson into children's past-life recall, but neither of these has any significant bearing on the full interlife experience. We should also remember that this was a pre-internet age when the sharing of research was considerably harder – especially in what were and still are regarded as fringe areas amongst most of the professional psychology community. Despite this it would still be possible to suggest that most of the pioneers were probably aware of each other's work, but did not deign to mention this fact in order to boost their own apparent contribution. But personal correspondence with a number of them has revealed that their research was indeed conducted totally independently of each other.

Finally we come to the issue of potential subjective leading by the therapists. Under hypnosis subjects tend to take instructions extremely literally, much like a computer program. This is exactly how pioneers like Whitton and Newton stumbled upon the interlife in the first place, because their imprecise commands led their subjects to enter a realm they had never previously encountered in a therapeutic setting – which in its own right meant they could not be leading them on, at least in the early stages of their research. So, at the very least, deliberate falsification of information is virtually impossible, unless the subject is not really in trance, and a skilled therapist can tell when that is the case. For the same reason subjects cannot just be told to experience something, because for the most part they have to be actually having the experience to report on it. On top of this, many of the transcripts of interlife regression sessions now available to us reveal that subjects are not mere automatons responding to suggestions. Instead they regularly scold or laugh at their interrogator's lack of understanding and if, for example, they are asked to move on from an element of the experience before they are ready, they will insist on delaying until they have finished with it to their own satisfaction. That is not to say that subjective leading is impossible, or never takes place – merely that it is far less common or possible than many skeptics would suggest.

For all these reasons, the underlying consistency of interlife testimony from what are now thousands of subjects would seem to give it a great deal of credibility. Indeed it is arguably the most profound source of spiritual wisdom that has ever been available to humanity. And its strength lies in its derivation from countless ordinary men and women, with no fixed preconceptions, no pretensions as spiritual gurus, and no political axe to grind.

Moving Into the Universal

In the Preface I discussed the background to my proposal that interlife research could be developed in a more universal direction to tackle broader questions of spiritual, historical and philosophical importance. But had this really not been attempted before? Newton, Modi and Cannon had all obtained some more universal information, but it would appear that they had gleaned this from their subjects as a by-product of the personal interlife approach. By contrast, Andy and I intended to break new ground by deliberately utilizing the way in which subjects can apparently enter into interactive, real-time discussions with their elders. As a result it would be the latter who would act as the prime source of information if the technique worked, rather than the subjects themselves. This would be a significantly different approach, with the potential for gleaning high-quality, consistent and more reliable information. Moreover, all three of the aforementioned pioneers had provided only scant data about their protocols – especially concerning the precise number of subjects involved, and the methods used to compare, analyze and present their data – which appeared to leave significant scope for improvement.

The other issue we discussed was whether this type of research might not be rather like the trance 'channeling' of entities from other realms performed regularly by mediums and other psychics – which we accept as having some validity, although simultaneously recognizing that it often produces information that appears rather less than reliable. Given our anticipation that our questions would be answered not so much by the subject's own higher soul-self but by their elders or similar, on the face of it we would be moving much more in this direction. But at the same time our research would be very different, for a number of reasons. First, we would be making the approach and setting the agenda – rather than our subjects merely acting as passive receptacles for whatever knowledge a supposedly higher source wanted to transmit. Second, our subjects would be chosen by Andy, and would not claim to have any special gifts or access to special channels of higher wisdom – they would be ordinary people with no pretensions, who happened to be best suited to enter the deeper states of trance required for this kind of work. Third, we would be obtaining information from multiple subjects and comparing them for consistency, not relying on one particular source of channeled material which could, even if broadly genuine, be highly subjectively influenced. And fourth, our interlife-based approach would involve subjects making contact with highly evolved souls that *by definition* must reside in the light realms – and everything we have learnt from interlife research suggests that such souls do not deliberately mislead or play tricks. So arguably it would be reasonable to assume that any information coming from them would be rather more reliable than that coming from traditional channeling entities, with their sometimes dubious claims as to who they are and in what plane they reside.

So it was that we came to the conclusion that we would be breaking substantially new ground if we undertook a properly planned and documented research program along these lines, which might provide us with reasonably reliable information of profound importance. So Andy began to identify suitable subjects, usually on the basis that he had worked with them successfully before. We refer to them using assumed first names only, to protect their anonymity, but their age, sex and country of residence are profiled in Appendix I. Meanwhile I produced a draft set of questions, concentrating on the following four areas that form the main chapter headings:

- unusual soul behavior
- soul development

- humanity's past and future
- reality and time

We spent a short time honing these to our mutual satisfaction, resulting in a final list of 21 primary and 50 secondary – or follow-up – questions, as shown in full in Appendix II, and then the research sessions began.

The Sources

Before we look at the results, it will be useful to say a few words about the sources with whom our subjects made contact. As already explained, our prior expectation was that they would connect up with their respective elders in order to answer our research questions. So when Andy felt each one was ready, he would ask them to 'go to the spirits of light that help you with reviews and planning'. He would then explain, for the benefit of the subject and any spirits of light in attendance, that we were undertaking some research for a book whose contents would be shared with the world.

As a result, five out of the ten subjects – that is Amy, Claire, Nadine, Naomi and Nora – did find themselves in the presence of their elders. But to our surprise the other five reported quite different presences, despite being asked to link up with their elders as usual. David reported that he met with certain 'wise ones' who were clearly different:

> There are five of them, but they seem quite different from the council... When I see the council, it usually feels solid as a temple. With these spirits it's very much an energetic environment... I just call them the 'wise ones'... I sense a greater love and understanding than the elders have. The love and compassion coming from them is extraordinary.

Katrine found herself with only one elder who was accompanied by a number of other spirits of light, who had apparently come together to help with our research. Alva described being in 'a gathering or special occasion, it's radiant, it's glowing, and there is a giant ball of very strong light'. And Veronica found herself in an entirely different environment again:

> I feel like I'm just floating in light... I don't feel like there are any spirits of light around me. I feel like I'm *in* them... This is where things just *are*, where healing just *is*, where knowledge just *is*.

Meanwhile Denise reported another unusual but not entirely dissimilar environment:

> This place is familiar but bewildering... It feels right though... It's not quite rooms but areas that are available to go into... I need to go into the third one... There is masses of information... I'm not communicating with a person, it is made up of many minds... It's like a classroom for teaching and learning. The room itself is what I'm talking to. It's like it's a vibrating wall of energy, and the information comes from all around.

Under questioning by Andy, Nora provided an interesting explanation for these more unusual sources of information – even though initially she only reported being in the presence of her elders:

> There is a special place to get information faster than going through the different council layers. It's just a place to tune in. And we only get information on a 'need to know' basis.

It was also encouraging to us, even if we cannot discount the possibility of conscious interference on the issue, that several of our subjects seemed to suggest that their sources were ready for our questions, and keen to be as helpful as possible. Nora, for example, reported that her elders were 'really interested – they say this is different'.

The Selection and Presentation of Transcript Material

With research sessions that each lasted several hours minimum, and some subjects needing more than one session to complete the questions, it will not be difficult to appreciate that we amassed a huge amount of research material. And while the entirety was painstakingly transcribed, to have presented it all would have made for a long and often incomprehensible book with no room for commentary. It was therefore necessary for me to make a number of decisions about how to select and then present appropriate extracts from the source material.

As far as selection is concerned I had to apply a number of criteria. These are discussed fully in Appendix I, but in summary I had to make judgments about whether answers were relevant, whether they made sense, and – most difficult of all – whether they appeared to be free of conscious interference. Like all expert therapists, Andy had mechanisms for maintaining a sufficient depth of trance that the potential for such interference from our subjects' conscious minds was minimized. But we should be aware that this is not an infallible process, so that other techniques must be applied to weed out potentially unreliable material. One was to attempt to establish the extent of prior knowledge of certain topics, and we subsequently asked our subjects whether they had read particular books that I regarded as being of particular relevance. The other was to ask them to identify any sections of their transcripts that surprised them, either because they contradicted previously held views or because they had no prior knowledge of the information they gave. We will see that all this information has been incorporated into the appropriate sections.

In any case, if our various controls have worked, for the majority of the time it should be our subjects' ethereal sources who are speaking in the pages that follow, and not our subjects themselves – and the regular emergence of profoundly wise and inspiring messages arguably supports this contention. But we have no names for our sources. We did not ask for such information, and they did not proffer it – indeed, we already knew that names mean nothing to true spirits of light. So when subjects' pseudonyms are used, it may be helpful if they are thought of as speaking on behalf of their sources, and not of themselves. To support this approach, from now on the word *subjects* is used only when strictly appropriate, while for the majority of the time the word *sources* is used instead.

Nevertheless, let us be clear that at no time did our subjects speak in anything other than their normal voices, albeit that as we would expect they sometimes spoke more slowly and quietly. So they were not in any way being 'taken over' by their sources, as is the case with some supposed mediumship or channeling.

If we turn now to presentation, subjects in trance vary in their eloquence. Some tend to labor points and repeat themselves at times, and their spoken grammar can leave something to be desired – especially if English is not their first language. So undue repetition, deviation or hesitation has been removed, and grammar has sometimes been improved. Moreover, in these research transcripts Andy's primary and even secondary questions tended to follow a relatively set pattern, and are reproduced in the section and sub-section headings. So for the most part only the subject's comments are reproduced, although the omission of any interventions by Andy has been marked with ellipses. But when there is a particularly revealing interaction, it is reproduced in full.

Above all, whatever adjustments have been made to the extracts from original transcripts, the objective throughout is to maintain their accuracy in terms of content and intent, but at the same time ensure they are concise and readable.

1

UNUSUAL SOUL BEHAVIOR

Our first group of questions deals with aspects of soul behavior that we have labeled 'unusual', although some are in fact more common than might normally be supposed. It includes topics such as trapped souls, attachments, soul fragmentation, multiple incarnations, walk-ins, imprints, traumatic body memories, suicide and demonic entities. Various spiritual commentators and regression pioneers have adopted different views about many of these, especially in the detail, meaning that no clear and consistent line of thought has previously existed. But the reliability and objectivity of our sources was arguably proved here more than in any other group, because they were unanimous in their answers to the eight out of nine primary questions that required only a yes or no answer – albeit that the secondary questions reveal added nuances. Nor were they always merely adopting the line taken in the most common potential source of prior knowledge for the subjects themselves – Michael Newton's work.

Trapped Energies, Fragments and Imprints

1.1 After physical death can soul energy fail to move into the light and become trapped in earth's astral plane?

Andy and I commenced with arguably the simplest and least controversial question. To clarify, while the difference between the physical plane and the light realms is reasonably obvious, the general consensus is that there is an intermediate state in which soul energy can remain trapped after death. We might refer to this as the *astral* plane, and it is generally thought of as having a close association with the physical. But we should be clear that it is not appropriate to think of either the astral or the light planes as having any sort of 'location' such as 'up there' and so on. Instead all three planes should be thought of as occupying the same 'universal space', but with different levels of energy vibration or frequency.

In any case, most people who believe in soul survival would answer this question in the affirmative. And this is, of course, what all of our sources did.

1.1.1 If so, why does this occur?

Again there were no major surprises when we asked why this might happen. Claire emphasized that 'strong emotions' play a major part, while Nora stressed the confusion that arises if the 'human rather than soul element remains dominant'. Denise similarly reported that such souls have 'just forgotten their connection, and do not carry the awareness held by the bigger part', while Naomi indicated that 'they are scared of the concept of death, and may still see themselves as being alive'. David expanded somewhat, as follows:

> It is triggered by strong emotions, or physical pain... This results in an inability to let go of that life, so that soul energy remains stuck in the heavy earth emotions and is not able to move away.

But probably the most complete and insightful explanation came from Veronica:

> It is because of a traumatic life or death, an unexpected death, or unresolved issues. Where there are very, very dense emotions it causes conflict and confusion for the soul. Although there is freedom and peace and love in the light, the soul is drawn to stay on the earth, because it's more comfortable to have such dense emotions in such a dense place than it is to bring them into the light and look at them properly.

1.1.2 Is it the entire soul energy that was originally brought down that becomes trapped, or merely a fragment?

We saw in the Introduction that we only bring a certain percentage of our soul energy into incarnation in the first place, so one would assume that this is the maximum amount that can remain trapped in the astral plane. But it also seems logical that only a fragment of this energy might remain trapped, with the rest being repatriated into the light as normal. As far as I am aware this is an issue that is not commonly discussed by other researchers.

Alva alone was adamant that it is always the entire soul energy brought down that remains trapped, while Naomi was marginally more flexible: 'It *can* divide, but it tends to stay together until it returns to the light.' However both Veronica and Katrine adopted the rather more fluid view that it can be a fragment of any size:

> There is often a small amount of soul energy left upon the earth when the majority has returned, and this can be as small as a thought or a feeling, perhaps left with somebody that the soul was close to. However there are also occasions when a lot more soul energy remains, and it is even possible for no soul energy at all to return to the spirit realm when a soul feels truly traumatized and detached from its source. Those are the souls who really need deep healing.

> It can be just fragments… When a soul experiences a traumatic death, if it is advanced it wouldn't be that damaged because it's not so confused when it leaves the body, so usually it would take more of its soul energy with it. But if it's a young soul who's very confused after leaving the body, they don't know what's going to happen and they can just get stuck there – they don't follow any light, or know where to go.

1.1.3 Will these energies always move into the light and be reunited in the end?

Our sources were unanimous that complete trapped spirits and major fragments are always repatriated with their core soul energy, whether after a long or a short interval – although remember we are speaking here from an earth-time perspective, whereas all discarnate soul energy whether trapped or not will have a totally different concept of time. As to how repatriation is achieved, according to Katrine, Denise and Amy it is by various combinations of assistance from the earth and light planes:

> Usually there would be teachers who would go and try to recover the soul from where it is… But if the help also comes from the earth plane it's much easier… It's easier to contact that part of the soul, because it's more connected to earth energies when it has just died.

> Help can come either from the earth or spirit planes… Spirit guides and other souls can be involved, or the soul itself can retrieve fragments left behind once awareness is reached on whatever plane. It will understand what has caused them to become separated, although they are still attached by a fine cord. They simply need to be recoiled, and brought back to the core soul energy.

> Trapped soul energies are given a lot of help… You can't do it from the earth plane without having help from the spirit realms.

Meanwhile Alva gave rather more unusual details of how, very occasionally, trapped energy can be so dense that it has to be 'reshaped' in some way, which does seem to echo one of Newton's findings:

The trapped element is never lost, there will always be a connection.
So will these energies always move to the light at some point?
Mostly, but not always.
Tell me about the times when they are not reunited with their own core.
The trapped energy needs to be reshaped. There are spiritual beings that will – not reform – but maybe connect it in a different pattern, so it's like a fresh start... It's like they send in little sparks of energy for the heaviness, to sort of offset it... They are very strong and powerful souls with extremely big hearts and a strong feeling of love for all. And with a lot of patience.
What sort of souls do they work with?
The very, very few that are so heavy that no one else can help. There are not many of them... They are people who have misused their power and strength, or that play with the dark sides – who are unbalanced between the light and the dark... Or people who have no contact with their feelings.
And once this energy is reworked, can it rejoin its own core soul?
Yes. It will always belong to its own energy, it will never disappear... The soul will always have a longing to be complete, and will feel incomplete without all of its energy. So when the heavy part is gradually getting lighter again, it will slowly be attracted to the original soul.
If a soul loses a fragment that remains earthbound, can it still reincarnate?
Yes... And if they then work with the light once back on the earth plane, that can attract the denser energy and it can be rejoined in that way.

However our sources were not so unanimous about whether smaller fragments have to be repatriated, as we are about to find out.

1.1.4 Is there a difference between a fragment and an imprint?

We have already seen that both Veronica and Katrine mention the idea of merely leaving behind tiny fragments such as isolated thoughts, feelings or emotions, and I had previously wondered whether there might not be a difference between smaller and larger fragments. I had dubbed the former 'imprints', assuming they would be more passive – for example, as characterized by spirit figures who are occasionally seen repeating the same repetitive walk or activity, in the same place, in an endless and unchanging cycle. By contrast I assumed that larger fragments would be more proactive as typified, for example, by poltergeist activity. Again, this is not something regularly discussed by other researchers as far as I am aware.

A number of our sources seemed to accept that imprints should be distinguished from fragments, the key difference for Nadine and Amy being that fragments have to be repatriated whereas mere imprints can just be left behind:

> Fragments and imprints are very similar, but they have different properties. Fragments are basically 'bits' that have been left behind and can be rejoined at a later stage. Imprints are basically like a carbon copy that has been left behind that still has information on it… Either unintentionally, or so others can connect with it… But in time they disappear.

> A fragment is the part of the reincarnating soul energy that remains. An imprint is just a memory in space… Like an emotion or a trauma… I think these can be left behind.

Similarly Katrine and Nora, although not distinguishing imprints specifically, both suggested that smaller fragments can be left behind:

> Fragments don't have to be reunited, but it would be best… The soul can manage without fragments, but it would take longer to develop because it's harder to go back and reincarnate if you don't have the whole soul to take energy from… It's like not having enough fuel, if you have a full tank it's much better.

> Souls can come back and collect fragments… If it's an energy that they need to keep working with. But if they have learned the lesson of that emotion then they can leave it where it is.

Meanwhile David appeared to accept that a distinction could be made between fragments and imprints, but for a different reason:

> Whereas fragments get stuck, an emotional imprint is left as a choice, but ultimately it is all part of the same energy.

But this is where we come to the first real disagreement between our sources, because he was also adamant that even such imprints must be repatriated with their core soul energy at some point. Veronica, Claire and Denise all seemed to share this view:

> Everything, even an emotion, is energy… Any energy that is left behind always has to be reunited with its core, although it may take time. It's all part of their energy. They're incomplete without it.

> Trapped soul energy of any size will always reunite with the energy

remaining in the spirit realms.

Even with an imprint there's still a connection.

What are we to make of this? One conclusion we can draw is that if mere emotional imprints *should* be distinguished from larger fragments, it *is* because they are not essential to the core soul and do not need to be repatriated. If on the other hand all energy fragments, however tiny, do need to be repatriated, then arguably there is no point in making the distinction in the first place – except perhaps to accept that from a human perspective larger fragments of trapped energy have the potential to be more proactive than smaller ones, which will tend to be more dormant.

In general I am intuitively attracted to the idea that some 'ghosts' are mere imprints or, to use Nadine's phrase, 'carbon copies', that can be left behind without affecting the originating soul's ability to carry on with its learning and growth. Nevertheless, we will find in the next two sections that the overwhelming view is that any energy 'lost' by the core soul in various different circumstances has to be repatriated sooner or later, no matter how small it may be, and this too has a certain resonance. On this issue, then, we will have to retain an open mind.

1.1.5 How often does this occur?

As far as fragments and imprints are concerned, Nadine, Katrine, Nora and Denise were unanimous that they can be left behind quite frequently, and no other source explicitly contradicted this view.

But when we turn to the far more contentious issue of how often the entire soul energy brought down remains trapped, again there was some disagreement. Amy was rather vague in reporting that 'every soul will have been stuck at one point, but it's a very individual thing'. But Claire, Nora and Denise were adamant that it is rare, proffering 'only a very, very small percentage, less than one percent', 'not very often, maybe two percent of the time or not even as much as that' and 'only rarely' respectively. By contrast, and in line with their earlier suggestions that it is always or normally the entire energy that remains trapped, Naomi suggested this happens 'frequently' and Alva 'quite often, with big groups of people wandering about in confusion, not knowing, in despair'

At this point it is probably important to provide some counterbalance to the proliferation of television shows in which mediums are used in attempts to contact and film trapped spirits. Because proactive, full, trapped spirits seem to lurk around every corner, viewers might easily be forgiven for assuming this must be the norm after death. But were this the case we might expect to find interlife regression subjects occasionally mentioning, for example, that one of their soul group members was absent because they were busy trying to appear on *Most Haunted*. Whereas in fact we never hear them talking about soul mates remaining trapped in the astral plane. This alone should be enough to suggest that the phenomenon is not particularly common, and by no means the norm.

Attachment of Trapped Energies

1.2 Can soul energy trapped on earth attach itself to other people?

Most researchers accept this idea, so again this was a relatively uncontentious primary question that received a unanimous yes from our sources.

1.2.1 If so, why does this occur?

There was little in the way of disagreement about why this occurs either, the consensus being that 'like attracts like'. Here are Amy, Alva, Nadine and Nora:

> Like attracts like, in temperament, in emotions and belief.

> If they find a vibration that matches theirs.

> If people have a frequency that is similar to or the same as theirs.

> They are attracted to the same energy. So if a person is working on anger, then that could attract trapped energy that is similar.

Katrine and Veronica agreed, emphasizing that such energies can also attach themselves to places or even objects:

> They find they are attracted to people with particular emotions or lifestyles, and they are looking for a home that is familiar… Or it can be a place or a building.

> There are times when they are drawn to a living energy, but they can also become attached to places and to objects. Where something feels safe, where something can give them energy or they can draw something from it, then they will invariably become drawn to it and attached.

However Naomi and Denise went one step further, making the intriguing suggestions that *opposites* can also attract:

> If there is fear in the host, an energy that is going to increase that fear will be attracted to it… If a spirit likes anger or violence or drinking or

terrorizing it can play that out in the host and feel comfortable. For the host it is an increased learning experience because of the added intensity, but at some point it will start to feel uncomfortable... Or, if there is a very confident host, the same fearful spirit can attach and that may still be a learning experience. For example, if a very fearful baby has died, it might look for the reassurance of a soothing mother. So it can be like with like or opposites.

They are searching for, and can only be attracted to, something or someone that resonates in a similar way. Or they might resonate with a place. And some trapped energies have many issues, not just one, and where they go depends on the strongest... But they might not only resonate with the same emotion, but also with its opposite. For example, if they had anger they could be attracted to someone who could not express their anger

1.2.2 What are the effects on the host?

Most answers to this question were relatively brief. For example, Amy merely said 'it attaches but it's still separate', while Claire asserted that 'they can exert an influence, but there is no joining'. Katrine expanded slightly: 'They cannot control the host, but they will have effects... On their emotions... On their way of thinking... They may even cause things like clumsiness or small accidents.' Denise was more explicit when she indicated that we should differentiate between single and multiple attachments: 'Some attachments may have no great effect but, when someone in a weakened state invites in many attachments without realizing, they can become overwhelmed.'

Nevertheless, it was again Veronica who provided the most detailed explanation when Andy asked her if there were different levels of attachment:

Some are fringe attachments, where the energy sits at the very outside of a person's energy system, where they just feel safe or are being healed because they are close to a loving, kind energy. But then there are other attachments that can be much deeper, where the soul energy almost feeds off the energy of the person or the place to whom they have become attached... They most commonly have an effect upon a person's health, because their energy is being disrupted. But there can be a merging of thought processes if the attachment is deep enough and has dense enough energies, so that the person they've attached to starts to experience the same patterns in life as those of the attachment. The energy has to be very strong, and there must be an opening, an opportunity, in order for it to be fully able to have an effect upon thoughts and behaviors. Most times there will only be a niggling thought on the outskirts of someone's mind, so they might feel drawn towards something they would not normally be drawn to, although it wouldn't be incredibly strong. But if they present the attachment with a large enough opening, they might be allowing that soul energy to really *live* through them, even to take over in some way.

1.2.3 Can this ever be planned?

When Andy asked Veronica if attachments serve some sort of purpose, she responded as follows:

It gives the attachment the opportunity to work through some issues that they haven't resolved. It's contentious, because it's not something that is agreed to be 'right', but at the same time it often has a beneficial outcome. Because the attachment is attracted to a host with similar issues, it can allow the host to work through some of its own issues as well.

Quite unexpectedly, this sounded as if attachments might even be planned in the spirit realms – and as far as I am aware this is not something regularly discussed by other researchers. So Andy probed her for more information:

It would not happen unless there was a mutually beneficial outcome. The choice is made on a soul level for this to take place. Because it's not a conscious choice, the living soul may feel invaded or violated, but on an unconscious level, somewhere along the line, this choice was made. The host soul may have stated at some point that it wanted to help another soul move on, or to help trapped spirits in some way, or to help someone with a trauma. And the attachment recognizes that that choice has been made. It would not be able to happen if there was not some form of consent somewhere along the line.

Naomi backed up this proposition:

A soul can enter another human body if it is invited in. Usually it is a joint decision on both sides, at a soul level.

Whether or not these two are right that *all* or at least *most* attachments are ultimately beneficial and preplanned, this is an interesting suggestion that I have not come across before. And I certainly accept that it could happen in *some* cases. Indeed, this was the arguably more balanced position presented by Katrine and Denise:

Sometimes it would be planned, but that doesn't happen often.

Sometimes it can be planned by both souls. But many humans resonate in such a way that they attract trapped soul energy without meaning to…

THE WISDOM OF THE SOUL

This happens when they don't use protection, and especially when their own energy field may have become open and weak through physical or mental illness, or worry. It has been a pattern for humans to ignore their full potential and power, and to consistently weaken their field.

1.2.4 How often does this occur?

Just as with trapped spirits, it is the extent to which attachments occur that is the really contentious issue. Some therapists, especially those who specialize in spirit release such as Edith Fiore and Shakuntala Modi, suggest that it is extremely common, but most regression pioneers tend to take the opposite view. So what did our research reveal?

Unfortunately our sources were equally split. At one end of the scale, Claire insisted it is 'a very small percentage, and not a common occurrence', backed up by Nora who declared 'it doesn't happen often, like one or two percent of the time, maybe even less'. In the middle sat Amy, who suggested 'it's more frequent than people realize'; Veronica, who said 'I'm getting the figure twelve percent'; and David, who reported 'it's not uncommon, but it's usually only temporary because there are forces at work on both sides to move the energies back to where they belong'. At the other end of the scale, Denise was adamant that 'the vast majority of humans will have one or more attachments at some points in their lives, although not all the time', backed up by Naomi and Alva who said it is 'very common' and 'frequent' respectively.

Again, what are we to make of this? It seems that the apparent confusion could have been caused by us not being sufficiently explicit about different levels of attachment. For example, we saw with the last question that partial soul fragments are left behind far more often than the entire soul energy brought down. So it is not inconceivable that deep attachments are relatively uncommon, but that fringe attachments occur rather more frequently.

1.2.5 What happens to the attachment when the host dies?

Although Nadine merely stated that attachments are 'washed away', the majority of our sources were unanimous that they might choose either to stay behind in the astral plane, or to travel to the light with their host. Here are Naomi, Nora, Amy, Alva, Denise and Veronica:

They can attach to another body, or they always have the option to go back to the light.

Often they look for another host that they are attracted to, but sometimes they move on into the light by themselves if there is nothing to link to.

They will generally stay where they are, attached to a place... Or they will find someone else that matches them... Sometimes they become ready to move on by themselves, but usually they are helped.

They can move on somewhere else or go into the light with the host... If so the attachment is split away automatically, and they go to their separate places of healing.

Depending on the circumstance, some choose to leave before death, some weaker ones cling to the energy at all costs, and some deliberately try to remain with the host's soul energy as it returns to the light, at which point there are those who will ensure that the attachment goes to the right place... As the energy leaves the human it crosses the veil, and when it comes through the other side the attachment will no longer be there. It's an automatic part of the crossover process that attachments are removed, and the soul involved may not even be aware that they had one.

The attached soul sometimes chooses to move with their host into the light, for the healing process. Usually, this would mean that they undergo healing of their issues as a knock-on effect of the healing of the host's issues, and would be able to return to their soul-source... But if the attached soul energy does not wish to go to the light, then they will detach from their host and may look for another host to attach to, or they may just stay upon the earth plane as a free soul energy for a while.

On the face of it these last three confirm my intuition, previously expressed in *The Book of the Soul*, that no attachment could remain with the host once it entered the light. They were also backed up by David, who reported that 'they go with the host, and this is part of the work of untangling energies and fragments'. However, Veronica herself added an interesting rider to this:

It has happened that there has been a choice for that attached soul energy to stay with the host, even into another incarnation... This might occur if there are karmic issues between them that can only be resolved in physical form.

Nevertheless, even if this observation is accurate, it seems likely that such behavior would be rare.

Finally, I have not mentioned the issue of possession because arguably this is merely another term for a deep attachment. There is of course the rather more contentious issue of *demonic* possession, but we will return to this topic in section 1.9.

Soul Fragmentation

Note that Veronica, Alva and Claire were not asked any of these questions.

1.3 Can we lose soul fragments while still incarnate?

The principle behind this question is that energy interactions between incarnate humans are complex, and some commentators suggest that certain intense, emotional interactions between two people can lead to soul fragments splitting off from one and attaching to the other, in just the same way as can happen with trapped soul energies. Our sources were again unanimous that this can occur.

1.3.1 If so, why does this occur?

The answers to this question were somewhat brief but to the point. Denise merely stated that 'this can happen in situations of severe loss, pain, trauma, fear or grief', with Naomi agreeing that 'the soul can fragment in times of trauma, confusion or upset'. Meanwhile Nora stressed that 'we don't always know we have lost something, it can happen automatically during certain episodes', and Amy that 'there has to be a connection with the other person, and their energy must somehow accept the attachment'.

1.3.2 Must these fragments rejoin the rest of the soul at some point?

There was a clear majority opinion that lost fragments do need to be repatriated, and that at the very least this is an automatic part of the transition into the light. Here is David:

> It's a common experience… But no soul fragments get lost. They may get stuck for a long time, but ultimately we know where all the fragments are… Usually they are retrieved when the soul enters the light without it even being aware of this.

The timing of this automatic process seems to present fewer problems than might be expected. On the one hand, if the 'host' who loses the fragments dies first, they can simply be retrieved from the 'recipient' who is still incarnate – whether automatically, or with deliberate effort from the host or their healers and guides. Or, if the recipient dies first, they could be detached at that point and reunited with that part of the host's soul that remains in the light realms.

Our other sources not only partially confirmed this, but also indicated that fragments can be retrieved while we are still incarnate – although interestingly they emphasized that all the impetus must come from the host, not from the recipient. Here are Nora, Denise and Katrine:

> The soul can retrieve it later if it needs to… Or, in incarnation, the person who lost it must have learned enough, or be strong enough, to have that bit back. It's not so important for the person it is left with.

> It can occur during the incarnation, consciously by the human, it can occur with help from another human, or it will be done when the soul returns… In incarnation it can be done in meditation or guided groups. You simply need to be in a relaxed open state, with the intent and focus to discover those moments when parts were lost, one at a time, and then find them because they will still be attached, and draw them back in… But your understanding must be of the *whole* situation or circumstance. There doesn't have to be forgiveness, that can create a barrier, and understanding will automatically lead to forgiveness… The process is reinforced if you have a visual image of the piece being returned.

> You don't lose soul energy by interactions. Another person can take energy from you… But it's only like your aura expands a long way from what you can see, so if you think about someone you will also send them energy automatically. But if you call the energy back it will come back... By the same token, with any energy from someone else that is attached to you, the other person has to recall it. But they have to want it, then usually that thought of wanting is enough... Or after death it can still be resolved. Their spirit guide will know what has happened and will send some help to the other soul so they can take it back, or just become aware that it's there.

From the perspective of the recipient rather than the host, we will shortly come to the issue of how to *avoid* picking up fragments of other people's energy. But these comments do seem to suggest that we should not be unduly concerned about any that we might have picked up *already*. I would support this view, provided on an emotional level one has 'let go' of the situation that caused any fragments to be transferred, and of the person to whom they belonged.

Meanwhile Nadine was again somewhat unusual as the only source to suggest that repatriation of lost fragments is merely optional:

> It depends on what the soul wants. If it wants to reclaim them, it can… Or it can leave them on earth in order to pick them up again when it reincarnates… Otherwise in time they just dissipate.

Although Naomi backed the general consensus by reporting that 'everything will be reunited eventually', she did seem to agree with Nadine's suggestion that fragments can be left behind deliberately to be worked on in a future incarnation:

> Parts can be lost but then reclaimed at a later stage, either in this life or another one. But they can also be attracted to another person, or they can remain in limbo.

Of course, once we enter the realm of emotional fragments being left behind for further work we should recognize two things. First, this would now be a deliberate choice by the discarnate soul. It seems it would be rather like selecting that emotional energy to bring back down, as we saw in the Introduction, except it would already be here on earth when they returned. Second, it would no longer be appropriate to think of that emotional fragment as being attached to the original recipient. The only rider to this is if, as with the idea of attached trapped soul energy mentioned by Veronica in the last section, there was a deliberate agreement for the recipient to carry that fragment through to another incarnation in which they would be working with the host.

1.3.3 What can we do to avoid losing or attracting soul fragments?

Katrine concentrated only on the issue of avoiding attraction, and suggested the standard approach of 'white light' protection. But Amy, although somewhat accepting of the inevitability of such energy interactions, attempted to look at both sides of the question:

> You can't avoid it. And it might be that you can be of some service to that other soul when it happens. By the same token you can't stop another person's emotional energy attaching itself to you, but you can minimize this by becoming as emotionally healthy as you can, and aware of the energy dynamics.

This general advice about awareness of energy dynamics appeared to be reinforced by David and Denise:

> By self-knowledge, understanding what's happening, and having support around to guide us. It's like most illnesses, if you can see what's happening at an early stage you do a lot of work quite quickly to redeem the situation, but if it's left untreated it takes a lot more effort.

> Live life with empowerment, and with a conscious awareness of the true situation and not just of the body.

Multiple Incarnations

1.4 Can a soul have two or more incarnations at the same time?

This is an idea often proposed by researchers, at least in part as a possible explanation when there appears to be an overlap between the dates of two incarnations. Having said that, documented cases of this are rare and imprints – which we will consider in section 1.6 – are in any case another potential explanation.

Nevertheless, we wanted to know what our sources would have to say about it. Again they were unanimous that it is indeed possible.

1.4.1 If so, why does this occur, and are there any risks?

They were also unanimous that this is usually done in an attempt to accelerate the learning process by working on two life issues at once. But they were equally agreed about the seemingly inevitable downsides. Here are Alva, Katrine, Amy and Claire:

> Souls have to divide their energy more than normal, so it's not recommended.

> It takes a lot of planning and organization with elders and guides... And they risk being exhausted.

> It is not encouraged, because you can only take a smaller amount of energy with you into each life, so it's better to be focused just on one.

> It is possible but it is not advised, because the intensity of emotions can cause confusion to the life's purpose.

Nadine, David, Denise, Veronica, Nora and Naomi supported these statements, but also mentioned that the level of experience of the soul is relevant to this issue:

> Their energy formation may not be strong enough to fulfill the intentions they have for both those body forms... It takes a very focused soul to be able to do this.

> Its purpose is to accelerate soul growth, but quite often it has a detrimental effect because of the lack of soul energy in each life. It's usually a path taken by emerging souls that have more confidence than experience. We never deny them the option, but we recommend against it... Because often such lives do not take the path expected.

> To accelerate learning some may wish to experience two very different, almost opposite, lives at the same time... But it is not encouraged... It

requires high energy… It's hard for each part of the soul to remember and stay strongly connected to its original intent… So it tends to be done by older souls.

Theoretically a soul might do this if it wishes to work on a number of issues, but it's not a choice that is encouraged… Younger souls may choose to incarnate into several forms and pick an issue for each to work on and develop, but those forms would be short-lived. There is more benefit in incarnating in one form and truly experiencing at a deep soul level than there is in incarnating in two forms and having minor experiences in each. Even the most enlightened souls who have reached a state of great clarity and purity still find it incredibly hard.

They can do that but they won't learn twice as much, they learn less effectively than having just one life… More evolved souls learn faster, and so don't have to experience so much to learn the same thing.

There are occasions when it is deemed to be a sensible and attractive option for a more advanced soul, but for most souls it is not because they will be tested more than they realize… It can mean that there is insufficient energy in the host body, so it can bring on more trauma and upset.

The clear consensus is that the use of multiple incarnations, although superficially attractive to less experienced souls who are in a hurry to learn, is far more appropriate for those with more experience. Veronica added that 'it's usually where there is something for that soul to *give* that it is more beneficial', which clearly relates to the idea of a more experienced soul having an altruistic life whose purpose is more to help other people's learning than its own. Claire explicitly corroborated this use of multiple incarnations:

It can happen if the purpose of one of the chosen lives is to help other souls with their lessons, so that one life is serving and the other is learning… Because the one of service does not require so much soul energy.

Meanwhile Veronica provided an additional, specific reason why highly evolved souls might sometimes have multiple incarnations:

There are some highly evolved souls who are not *required* to incarnate for their own development but may *choose* to incarnate if they feel it would be beneficial to the development of all. And they may choose to split their energy and incarnate in two separate parts of the world at the same time to bring their particular loving, healing energy to those areas.

Andy also asked Denise if it would be possible for a soul to have more than two incarnations at the same time, but unsurprisingly she was adamant that this would be unlikely because 'any more than two would dissipate the energy too much'. Alva agreed with her:

> It has been tried, but without much success. It's like digging little holes all over the place without getting much out of it.

1.4.2 How often does this occur?

Most of our sources who were asked how commonly this option is used seemed to suggest that it was rare. Alva, Nadine and Nora proffered 'not very often', 'not frequent at all' and 'maybe one in thirty' respectively, backed up by Veronica:

> A very small amount, less than one percent. With the level of work that needs to be done at the moment, souls are feeling there is more benefit, more to be gained, by putting a large amount of soul energy into one form… But everything is choice.

David was unspecific but, in line with the majority view that inexperienced souls may regularly try to take this option in defiance of any advice, indicated that 'it occurs more often than we would really like'. However only Katrine was significantly at odds with the others, reporting a far higher figure of 'maybe twenty percent'.

Walk-Ins

Note that Katrine was not asked any of these questions.

1.5 Can a soul vacate its adult body so another soul can walk in?

This is a highly contentious issue. The idea is that a soul can decide to vacate an adult body, perhaps because they are close to suicide anyway, and allow another soul to take their place so as not to waste the opportunities presented by that body. In other words, there is a complete swap. A number of commentators insist that it is possible, including the interlife pioneer Dolores Cannon. But others, like Newton, maintain that it is a nonsense – his key argument being that it goes against all ideas of personal karmic responsibility for the life contract we have taken on. But in addition, as we will see in section 3.3, to suggest that there is somehow a shortage of bodies for souls to incarnate into goes against all the available evidence.

So what did our sources make of this issue? They were, once again, unanimous that walk-ins do not take place.

1.5.1 If not, why not?

They were also unanimous about the reasons why they do not. Nora was somewhat reticent, merely indicating that 'the whole soul would not leave, there would always be something left, so there could never be a complete swap'. But a number of the others confirmed Newton's idea that the merger of any given body and soul is unique, and must take place in the womb. As a result they also insisted that if a soul leaves its body, that body dies, pure and simple. Here are Alva, David, Amy and Nadine:

> The soul has chosen that body, and it couldn't leave without the body dying as well.

> The bond between soul and body is too strong, and this would have the potential to destroy the body.

> What would be the purpose of that? A soul can only join while the baby is in the womb, and it takes the full time in the womb to make the connections between the soul and the body. So it cannot be done at any other time. And if a soul walks out, the body dies.

> When a soul has entered the baby, they've already reconfigured their energy into the energy of that baby, and so they meld into one. If the soul were to vacate, then that vacation would cause the person illness and death. For another soul to come in would be quite impossible, because the imprints of the other are still in there.

Claire, Naomi and Veronica were somewhat more circumspect, but still essentially in agreement:

> It is unlikely and difficult because each soul has a unique energy fingerprint that melds with the biochemical environment.

> It's a possibility but it rarely occurs... It would cause enormous difficulties, like intense neural dysfunction or mental incapacity.

> Anything is possible. But it would cause such a disruption that it wouldn't benefit anyone... Because the soul energies would be different. The problem would be magnified millions of times from the health and emotional problems caused by a mere attachment. So it is possible, but it would be very difficult.

Andy then pressed Veronica as to whether this was something that had ever happened in the past. She came up with an interesting suggestion that may tie in with the idea of early soul experiments on earth, which we will come back to in section 3.1:

> There were experiments when the human form was evolving, not maliciously but purely to understand how soul energy could live in such dense form. And it was found to be inadvisable. And in any case there are other ways of accomplishing a soul's incarnation, without disrupting the physical form in that way… So while this has happened in the past, it does not now.

Finally Denise went off on a somewhat different but nevertheless interesting tack, revealing some ideas about gaining guidance and assistance from another soul while still incarnate – which, she reported to us subsequently, she had never consciously read about or considered:

> A soul can choose to invite another in *without vacating*, for guidance... The visitor is consciously controlled by the host, who must invite it in, and usually this only happens for short periods of time and for mutual benefit.
>
> *Could anyone invite another soul down during a meditation?*
>
> Yes. People do it with their spirit guides.
>
> *How would that help the host, rather than intuitively linking?*
>
> Because there is a stronger connection. And also the visitor might like to just come down for a moment and enjoy the experience of the world – the sun, the wind, the rain, or the scenery if a nice place is chosen… Usually you would meet the spirit first to check that it was ok, you would be given guidance. You would usually ask if there was a specific question or problem, the answer would be stronger, and then afterwards the spirit is released… But it's essentially no different from any other form of guidance.
>
> *Do the two souls need to have an energy connection?*
>
> Yes, it will have been made before incarnation. Each person on earth has the ability to connect with the spirit that is right for them. But this can only be done with positive spiritual or personal intent, otherwise humans might invite in others with a lower vibration.
>
> *Is this an opportunity that is far more widely available than people realize?*
>
> You don't ask, even though you are always being told to! People don't stop to think about the possibilities. They are so concerned with their worries they create a spiritual fog.

Shared Soul Memories and Projections

1.6 Can a soul experience the complete past life of another soul?

The idea being explored here is that a soul can tap into any past-life memory of any other soul in the light realms, usually if there is something it can experience from it that will contribute to its learning and growth. Cannon is the only regression pioneer to mention this explicitly, and she refers to it as 'imprinting' – although so as not to confuse this with the energy imprints discussed in section 1.1, we now use the term 'shared soul memories'. However this idea is also clearly implicit in Newton's reports of soul mates replaying their past lives together.

So again it came as no surprise when our sources unanimously confirmed that it is indeed possible for souls to share all past-life memories. But before we continue it is important to remind ourselves that we have direct proof that at least some past lives are connected to us as individual reincarnating souls, rather than coming from a universal memory or consciousness. This is partly demonstrated by individual and specific karmic patterns and links – albeit that these could also be present to some extent in shared memories. But it is proven beyond doubt, as we saw in the Introduction, by children who carry over physical birthmarks or defects from their last life that exactly correspond to the wounds that killed their previous personality. We will see shortly that our sources confirm that *most* past lives belong to us as individual souls.

1.6.1 If so, why does this occur?

Claire, David and Veronica all confirmed that the purpose of sharing memories is to assist learning:

> It happens in the spirit realms… It allows souls to learn from each other's experience.

> It's for learning. It's like in the place of life selection, you can go in and join a body there and relive any life that's ever been lived to gain an insight. It's not exactly an imprint as much as a sharing of memories.

> Where an understanding of another soul's journey is required, and where it is appropriate for that to take place, then it could provide great insights and understanding.

1.6.2 Is there any essential difference between a shared soul memory and a genuine life of our own in the physical plane?

This far more interesting aspect is not even discussed by Cannon. Of course we would expect there to be a difference, otherwise there would be little point in going to all the trouble of having new lives of our own. Naomi, Katrine, Amy, Nora and Alva all corroborated this view, mostly from the primary question alone and with no further prompting:

> Experience is a very loaded word. They can visualize and be aware of another soul's past life, but it's not the same as living it. It's more like watching a film.

> They will not experience the whole life, but they can get the learnings and feelings from it.

> Your own past lives are right in the centre of yourself, whereas the others are more on the outside, in the mental realms only.

> We often talk about different lives up here, sometimes just little bits of them, sometimes we look at the whole thing. But we learn best by doing it ourselves… This is because you have to really experience the emotions… From the spirit plane it's not as complete, it's on a different energy level.

> They can sense the energy to learn from it, but they can't actually relive someone else's life.

We will find in due course that these views are essential to some of the more complex ideas we will be discussing in section 4.2. We might also note that Alva added 'because we all come from the same Oneness, we will always have fragments of everyone else's experience with us'. This is a separate although not entirely unrelated idea that we will follow up in section 2.3.

1.6.3 Would a regression subject be able to tell the difference between their own and other people's past lives?

It is probably safe to assume that at a soul level we can tell the difference between our own lives and shared memories – and Veronica, Nora and Alva all confirmed this in passing. But what about while we are incarnate, for example under regression?

Nadine indicated that a shared memory has a 'different energy frequency', although it was not made clear whether this could be picked up while we are incarnate. Meanwhile Denise was adamant that the distinction would be understood, even on the physical plane:

> On earth the person will remember and know the difference. If the intent is to regress to one of their own past lives, that is what they will do.

But Veronica suggested that the picture is not so clear-cut:

> It depends on how well they know their own energies and the experience of a regression. There are ways to tell… If it was for the purpose of understanding another soul's journey, the feelings may not be quite as

deep as when experiencing their own past lives. But if it was for healing, they would experience it as if it was their own.

Unfortunately this differentiation between understanding and healing is not clarified, but it seems likely that it leads us into the next area of discussion.

1.6.4 Can past-life regression sessions include 'projections' to help our learning or healing?

The issue of the extent to which lives recalled under regression may not even be someone else's, but projections concocted from a combination of either our own or other souls' lives, is relatively unexplored. Claire merely stated that 'to be aware that projection is possible is important'. But Katrine, Nora and Amy all provided further details about why projections are sometimes used:

> If the soul has difficulties in integrating with the body or brain of that person we can create a story for them to get learnings, because not everybody can experience a past life without a little bit of help. Or, because some people have many lives learning about the same thing, if they didn't have a single past life that was clear enough to make it understood, again we would make an appropriate life up.

> Most past lives that people experience are their own, except if they need to see something from another angle that they haven't experienced themselves... Then a spirit guide could project that down for them... Some of the basic lessons need to be seen many times from many different angles.

> True past lives are the ones that are felt and experienced, because the person has been involved in them. The others are only there to help them to understand a problem, and a possible future solution to it. But even these may be amalgamated into a true past-life experience.

Meanwhile Naomi's report that 'it is common to experience the past life of a spirit attachment' is worth noting, even if not directly relevant.

Carrying Over Body Traumas and Physical Characteristics

1.7 Can physical characteristics be carried from one life to another?

We saw in the Introduction and in the last section that Ian Stevenson's work with children who spontaneously remember past lives involves some cases where birthmarks or other defects exactly correspond to the wounds that killed their previous personality, and which have been substantiated by other obscure and verifiable evidence. So we were interested to see what our sources might have to say about the whole issue of carrying physical characteristics over from one life to another. And again they all agreed that this was possible.

1.7.1 Can traumatic body memories be carried over?

Perhaps more revealing was that a number of our sources focused on the issue of traumatic body memories, despite our subjects subsequently confirming that they had never come across this idea before, in Stevenson's work or elsewhere. Here are Naomi, Katrine, Amy and Veronica:

> Physical deformities can be passed from one life to another, until they are healed at a soul level.

> It might happen if there has been a wound or something that happened to the body and it has not healed in the spirit realms... It is to remind that person of unfinished business... It usually happens if you have the same learnings for a few lifetimes.

> They act as a physical reminder, on an unconscious level, of the lessons they're dealing with in the physical... It sets into play a repeat of the dynamic that happened with the original wounding. It doesn't necessarily have to be conscious, because the unconscious is creating or motivating the situation. Many people don't know and aren't aware that they're repeating the past.

> They are only carried forward if they involve an issue that requires healing... It may be a karmic issue and the purpose of incarnation is to clear it. It will have received healing in the spirit realms, and is unlikely to come through to another incarnation in quite the same way. For example, if a limb had been crushed in one life, it doesn't necessarily mean that in the next life the form will start with a crushed limb, but it may be that that limb is weaker, or develops aches or physical conditions, so that it can be used as a bridge to access the issues that need dealing with.

Meanwhile Claire, David, Nora and Alva corroborated these views, although subsequently confirming they had some prior knowledge:

> It's not normally intentional, but it can happen if there is incomplete cleansing of the energy body so that some remnant remains.

It generally happens with younger souls who have had a particular emotional trauma involving a primary emotion such as anger, fear, revenge or pain that has been carried over to the next life. They may have scars or deformations that act as a reminder – although I'm not sure it's a totally necessary reminder – but it's what that soul has chosen to do. But this goes against what we try and show about letting go... So we try and show them why it is not necessary, but ultimately they have to learn from experience, even if they do things that we may think of as mistakes on the way.

They are a reminder to give them a link to their memories of a particular learning, in the hope that they won't have to go through it again.

The physical marks mostly come through because they have been in a bit of a hurry to come back. They could have stayed on a bit longer in the spirit realms and had their whole energy field restored... So they act as a reminder that they should think about their choices a bit more. They haven't taken enough time to integrate, so they're just jumping into a new form to continue... The scars appear as physical on earth, but they are really a scar on the etheric body that hasn't healed properly.

Whether our subjects had prior knowledge of Stevenson's work or not, in discussing the *reasons* for carrying over traumatic body memories they were certainly going far beyond his self-imposed remit. And their reports do seem to confirm the suspicions I voiced in *The Book of the Soul* that these physical carry-overs might be intended to act as a reminder of incomplete emotional business, and that this would only involve relatively inexperienced souls who, in their hurry to return, had received insufficient healing. However Nadine and Denise seemed to suggest that the souls involved may have been making deliberate choices to do more work with certain emotions on the earth plane:

When someone has been wounded or hurt, the energetic imprint is inside their bodies. The soul can choose to take that memory back with them when they reincarnate, or to leave it in the spirit plane.

Some may choose this as a reminder, while others may choose less physical reminders.

We will return to the extent to which deliberate choice is involved in carrying over emotions or even physical reminders in the next chapter.

1.7.2 Can facial features be carried over?

The majority of our sources agreed that this too is possible. Naomi reported that 'physical characteristics are often chosen by the host, if they are things that make them feel comfortable', while Alva specifically concentrated on 'scars and lines'. But most of our sources agreed that, again, these are usually carried over to act as some sort of reminder for the person involved, or to act as a trigger for someone else to recognize them. Here are David, Veronica, Nora and Denise:

> Again it would be as a reminder, but there is less energy attached.

> It's generally a choice that is again used as a reminder. If there is a need for that soul's energy to be recognized on the earth plane, then physical attributes may be similar in each incarnation.

> Sometimes if people really need help to recognize someone they really need to meet. It's just to make the process easier.

> Some choose to simply because they can, or for more specific reasons – for example, it may be a trigger.

By contrast, Amy and Nadine stressed that more subtle recognition mechanisms tend to be more appropriate:

> Some things might be there to help you to recognize a person physically, but usually the recognition will be more challenging... The soul's energy can create the illusion, and many times people will recognize another familiar soul via their eyes. Then it's not a physical change, it's more like a hologram, it just changes what appears. And you might choose a personality that has familiar characteristics.

> This is a little bit complicated. The expression within the energetic soul of the person can actually change the face to make it suit the actual energetic information inside that soul. So the perception is that it looks like that, even though it doesn't in the actual physical matter of that body... It might be for recognition, in order for a karmic reaction when they want to relate to another incarnating soul in an energetic way, so they would remember. Or it might be to finish some learning or intent that hadn't been finished.

Meanwhile Katrine, although agreeing that facial features can be carried over, was somewhat on her own in her insistence that 'it doesn't happen very often, and it doesn't serve a purpose'.

1.7.3 How does this process work?

All our sources agreed that the process of carrying over physical characteristics, be they traumatic body memories or facial features, is effectively automatic – and from a soul perspective requires little or no effort. Here are Naomi, Alva, Veronica, Katrine, Nora, Amy and Denise:

Everything on earth is governed beautifully by the Source, so it will work out that the parents will have the right genetics and other characteristics.

The soul memory will go into the whole energy field of the baby... The human body is just an expression of what is in the energy field of the soul.

When a soul chooses its form for incarnation, that choice covers everything: their parents, and how their DNA interacts to become the DNA of the fetus. It's just that if that is what is required, that is what happens. It's an amazing synchronization of many energetic factors... This takes place before conception, it's in place from the moment the thought of that incarnation comes into being, it only takes a fraction of a second. But it would take infinity to truly understand in a scientific way, or to explain piece by piece, point by point.

It comes from the parents, but that is also part of the plan. So when we plan, we carefully review that family's DNA, so that will affect the baby and the soul... And it will be there when it starts to grow in the womb. It will be there before the soul joins.

It's all just energy, so whatever needs to be changed can be changed from up here. If the need is strong enough then the energy will be strong enough to make the change, and someone else up here sorts it out. It's like a little package of energy that travels with the soul energy and changes the physical, but the soul itself isn't always aware of this otherwise they might know too much... It has to happen early enough in the development of the baby.

The propensity's already there, the awareness is already there, it's part of the ingredient... Because you can see ahead. You've already decided the genetic makeup of the child, you've already decided its propensity for mental thinking and intelligence levels, you've already decided all the essential ingredients for the life and the challenges that you need. And that includes physical traumas, physical deformities, and minor physical attributes. All of that is chosen, that's already the physical future of that person... So everything is already in place when the soul is merging with the child.

It works via conscious thought manifesting the desired characteristic onto the energetic blueprint. There is an alignment before the physical creation, before fertilization, so nothing is altered, it just *is*. The necessary components in the male and female combine, it's all worked out in advance, it's already there in the energy.

Death-points and Suicides

1.8 To what extent is the death-point preplanned?

We saw in the Introduction that more experienced souls regularly choose to have an altruistic life, often of relatively short duration, in which the lessons are not for them but those close to them. We also saw that life planning in the light realms involves the examination of major probabilities and lesser possibilities. So in these exceptional cases it seems that the early death would have been a major, major probability, to such an extent as to almost render it a certainty.

But most aspects of most lives are far less predictable, and far more subject to the individual's own free will. Nevertheless, one issue that fascinates many people is whether their own death-point is already known in advance. Given that this is a major and indeed inescapable part of any incarnation, we felt it would be interesting to see what our sources had to say on the matter.

By far the majority view was that the death-point is no different to any other aspect of a life, in that there are elements of planning, but they can be significantly affected by free will. To get us started, here are Katrine, Claire and Naomi:

> Like everything else about the life, the death-point is planned, but free will always affects it too.

> There is the possible and the probable, but because of free will there is also always the possibility of change.

> A number of death-points are planned... If everything was preordained there would be no choice. So a number of options are preplanned based on the choices the person might take once incarnate.

However a number of our sources also mentioned the importance of the person completing their life lessons. Here are Nora, Nadine and Amy:

> It's a question of when the soul is ready to move on.

> When a soul incarnates, there is a point when they feel their intent has been fulfilled and that is the point when they feel they can leave the body. However they can exit at any time throughout their life, it depends on what the circumstances are and how they cope with what they set themselves. So the intent is already set, but free will has its way whenever it wants to.

> It depends on the individual's life and their circumstances and life

lessons. There may be one or two points in that life when the lessons have been learned.

David expanded on this point, indicating that the key is for us to be open and intuitively connected to our higher soul-self, so that when the right moment for death comes we are ready and do not resist it:

There are nearly always a number of death-points. But ultimately free will is always involved, and if somebody in incarnation is determined on a certain path then that can end in premature death, which has an impact on all those around them... They aren't usually remembered, but for many there are triggers. If the death is at the right point, due to age or illness, then the individual should know and be able to let go easily. But often what happens is that death is surrounded by fear and sometimes pain, so the signals get lost... Also if there is a sense of failure or incompleteness then it is harder to let go, whereas if all of the objectives have been reached then the ending is easier.

This idea that we should accept and be ready for death when the time is right is massively important, especially in the modern world when we seem to be increasingly obsessed by prolonging life at all costs, irrespective of its quality. I would add that merely accepting the reality of a spiritual worldview, and even more so of reincarnation, should go a long way towards reducing the fear of death and the fanatical pursuit of longevity.

Meanwhile Veronica provided the subtle and intriguing suggestion – which is clearly applicable to all aspects of incarnation and not just death – that even though free will reigns supreme, no choices are completely unforeseen:

It is preplanned to the same extent that the life is preplanned, in such a way that it's what is needed as a natural conclusion to that life. But there is always free will, and the practicality of how it occurs depends upon the free will that has taken the person to that point. So if a cathartic release is needed, it may be that they are standing in the middle of the road and they get hit. Or if their journey has brought them to a point where they are in a back alley, then it may be that they are beaten. But it is a cathartic death either way... There are no real accidents, only what are perceived as accidents when in physical form. Everything is choice, be it on a soul level or a conscious level. There is purpose in everything.

1.8.1 How are suicides viewed in the light realms?

A number of regression pioneers agree that suicide is probably more frowned upon than anything else in the light realms, because it involves 'breaking the life contract'. But our sources' initial responses to this question were somewhat mixed. Denise preferred to emphasize the help and guidance that would be provided:

> They need more help and guidance than most... A suicide is committed in times of deep pain and unclear thought, and this carries through into the spirit realm. Some suicides may believe in a better place when they die, but others may think everything is hopeless so they create the same on the other side. They will need retrieving from there so they can get the healing they need. It is the same as being stuck.

Alva backed this up by reporting that suicides 'need a lot of healing'. But Nadine reported that they are 'questioned', while David indicated that they are viewed with 'a sense of disappointment'. Nevertheless these two both went on to discuss the plans that would be made to provide sufficient support to resolve the situation, backed up by Denise:

> The next life would be planned so that the soul could actually cope in order to move on and learn that lesson, without going through the route of trying to go back home.

> It's something that we tolerate occasionally, but if it becomes a pattern then steps need to be taken... They might be moved to an easier world. Or they might have more extensive periods of meditation and teaching between lives. Or they might be given an easy life the next time round, with more support. The goal is to help them to understand how valuable the gift of human life is.

> They have a process of learning and explanation and reminding so they can make a choice themselves. Then in reincarnation they are given choices and chances, although if they persist they may still ultimately commit suicide. But each time the help given is stronger, and the efforts are more concentrated, and even more so in each spirit interlude.

It has to be said that none of this sounds unduly harsh, which is in line with what I would have intuitively expected. But what about souls who repeatedly commit suicide? Denise has just indicated that increasing help is given, and both Alva and Naomi emphasize that this is viewed with just as much equanimity – while both agreeing that the problem often lies in bringing too little soul energy into incarnation:

> It's not much different from many other soul experiences. When there is a lower amount of soul energy, they might not have the strength to make the right choices.

If a repeating pattern emerges they get increasing help from their spirit guide. They may choose more supportive family environments, or to take more soul energy with them into incarnation.

Andy also returned to this issue incidentally with Denise at a later point, and she suggested that an interesting additional option would be available to a soul who repeatedly struggled with physical life and kept committing suicide:

It depends on each individual. Some choose to stay in confusion, some will wish to return to a simpler incarnation... Either way appropriate help will be given in spirit or on earth. The choices are still the same, but the energy may need recharging. However some choose not to carry on and return to the Source... They can choose just to stay there, or they may experience such a high vibration it will give them the push to want to become separate again.

This idea of effectively opting out and returning to the Source early is one we will return to in section 2.1. But for now those who have been conditioned to view this as the ultimate goal might note that Denise describes it with relative indifference.

The other issue with suicide is, of course, the attitude towards it when someone has a serious and debilitating illness. It will come as no surprise that this is regarded as even less of a problem. Here, for example, is Katrine:

If someone has been suffering long-term illness or something like that, then it's about learnings... If the body can't take it any more, and the soul really, really wants to go, then it's ok.

1.8.2 Are suicides ever preplanned?

This question has not really been considered by Newton or any of the other pioneers, but not only was Veronica conciliatory about suicide but she also expressed the view that it can be a useful part of experience:

Although it is a difficult choice to make and may not be quite what was intended, it may be what was needed... Whatever happens in physical incarnation is viewed as a learning development, and is treated as such in the spirit realms. There is no judgment, because we do not feel those things, and suicide may be the experience that was required.

Alva seemed to support this view when she reported that 'some people might have to experience suicide'. As for whether suicides can be deliberately preplanned to assist others, our sources agreed that they can be, although most suggested that it would only happen rarely, and their reasoning varied. David and Claire made the obvious point that it would only form part of a lesson for others who were close to that person, but Alva added that the experience can be useful to 'take back to others in the spirit realms'. Meanwhile Nadine suggested it would only happen 'if they have a karmic objective that was agreed by their soul group'. Taking this idea a stage further, Amy and Katrine both agreed it would only involve a large number of souls, with the latter citing those who might plan to be the victims of 'natural disasters or something' – although they also correctly pointed out that these are not really suicides at all.

Demonic Beings

1.9 Are there any real demonic beings?

The final question in this group is arguably the most controversial of them all. The majority of the pioneering interlife therapists reject the possibility of any sort of hell or demonic beings, at least in part because of the compelling testimony of a number of their subjects when asked to comment on the issue. Nevertheless, Modi not only believes in their existence but asserts that demonic possession is occurring on a frightening scale, and in the broader community she is not alone. Supporters of this view also insist that the complacency of those who dismiss such entities plays right into their hands. So this is a debate that can become somewhat heated, and we were particularly eager to see what our sources would make of it.

Superficially they were again unanimous in rejecting the existence of demonic beings, and several of them laughed openly when asked the question. But on deeper probing it became clear that the issue is rather more complex. The majority emphasized that the human race has invested so much psychic energy in thoughts and fears of such beings over the millennia, encouraged by various religious institutions, that they have indeed given them a degree of autonomous existence. Here are David, Claire, Denise and Nadine:

There are those that pretend to be... But they are just delusions created by man.

They are created on the earth plane, almost like a thought-form.

If that is how people wish to see them, that is how they will see them...
As ever they can be created by conscious, human thought... But they can

then be embellished or enhanced and their energy can grow.

Demonic beings are not beings at all. They are brought to life by human minds, and so have been allowed to come into existence. You can create any energy form you want, be it positive or negative.

But the key point, emphasized by Nadine, is that 'in essence, they do not exist'. In other words, it seems likely that if the human race cut off their psychic energy supply, they would fade and die. Meanwhile Amy was unique in proffering the idea that trapped spirits could project themselves as demonic to avoid being moved on:

What people experience as demonic is their own fears. Or it can be that souls are trapped on the earth plane, and their only recourse to protect themselves from being moved on is by projecting thoughts of fear and things that might be perceived as demonic.

This could perhaps provide an explanation for the accounts of possessed people requiring exorcism that have received widespread attention in films and the media, which I am not inclined to reject in their entirety. But it also raises a wider possibility. Many spiritual travelers claim to have encountered hellish realms, particularly in modern times under the influence of psychedelics. Might these not be merely aspects of the astral or 'lower' plane? After all, at least one characteristic of this is that it is inhabited by trapped souls who remain to a greater or lesser extent tortured by unresolved emotions and attachments to the physical, and fail to realize their true soul nature.

1.9.1 If not, are there any non-human 'dark forces' acting outside of the 'plan'?

There are many spiritual commentators with no particular religious affiliations who insist that at the very least there are 'dark forces' inhabiting other worlds who attempt to influence, and are a threat to, the human race – even if they would not go as far as to label them demonic. Of course at the heart of this view lies the whole issue of 'good versus evil'. But Veronica and Katrine were adamant that dark and light are merely two sides of one coin – and even that they are only human perceptions that disappear once the bigger picture is understood at a soul level:

Dark is a perception... All energy is spirit, and all spirit is energy... So every energy form works towards the overall plan. Good and evil are perceptions. Dark and light are perceptions. They are all the same, without one there would not be the other. They are all different viewpoints.

There is light and dark, but the dark is not demonic, it comes from the light... There is no evil. All souls come from the same place.

Of course, some people can be easily offended by the suggestion that there is no such thing as evil, but I should stress that in supporting it I am not adopting a trendy position of moral relativism just for the sake of it. Instead I am following the lead of our sources, and attempting to evaluate the issue from the soul rather than the human perspective.

So it is clear that much of what we as humans might perceive as dark or even demonic forces are merely our own creations or misconceptions. But there is still a crucial question that remains. Are there any genuinely independent and objective entities of one sort or another that exist in other realms, whether initially created by our own psychic projections or not, who can and do influence events on the earth plane for the worse? Who – even if we acknowledge the fact that all soul energy originally comes from the Source – are effectively working outside of 'the plan', and creating at least an earth experience that is in some way an 'aberration'? Here are some further reflections from Alva, David, Nora and Naomi:

There is a struggle between light and dark, but there are no dark forces as such.

There are darker energies that are not too concerned about frightening others… They are souls who have chosen that path in order to learn about themselves, and in order to teach others about that particular way... But it's all part of the scheme.

I don't think there are any things on earth that are not there for souls to learn.

Everything comes from one Source, but energy can change its form. And bad energy attracts other negative energy, so you can have energy 'pulls' which create negative energy and can linger in a bundle or a thread, which then attracts its like as it floats through earth space... So there is negative energy that can be perceived as demonic, and there can be very destructive forces. But it is only negative energy. It does not come from a different Source.

It would probably be a mistake to be too dogmatic about this, but generally speaking it seems our sources are adamant that nothing exists outside of the overall plan. So I would suggest that the conclusion to be drawn is not that we should be complacent and assume everything in the garden is rosy. As we will find in section 3.4, humanity is clearly at a crossroads, both in terms of its own spiritual evolution and of what we are doing to our planet. However the message from our sources does appear to be that we should concentrate on taking responsibility for this ourselves, rather than on trying to blame it on supposed outside influences. As for the rather more far-reaching suggestion that the whole earth experience is an illusion and aberration set up by fallen angels of some sort, we will return to this in section 2.1.

2

SOUL DEVELOPMENT

Our second group of questions concerns the whole issue of how souls develop. To that extent it encompasses topics such as the purpose of reincarnation, the differences between human and animal souls, how souls are created, how souls use their time in the interlife, the roles they adopt once they no longer need to reincarnate, and other planets or dimensions and their inhabitants. Although we are no longer dealing with simple primary questions requiring a yes or no answer, there is still considerable agreement amongst our sources on most of these issues, albeit again with some differences at the secondary level. We will also find that they consistently contradict most of the central assumptions that underlie the various traditional religions and other spiritual or mystical approaches – even those that are based on the principle of reincarnation.

The Purpose of Reincarnation

2.1 What is the purpose of reincarnating on the physical plane?

A brief glance back through their responses in the previous chapter will show that our sources repeatedly referred to 'learnings', as they did throughout their research sessions. But in response to this question they were even more specific in consistently confirming my central theme in *The Book of the Soul*, which is that the underlying karmic dynamic for *all* souls – without exception – is one of learning, experience and growth.

The brief but apposite response from Denise was 'experience and learning'; from David, 'to learn, grow and understand'; from Katrine, 'we have to learn'; from Naomi, 'each soul is aiming to learn and grow as much as it can'; and from Nora, 'there are so many lessons to be learned about human feelings and so on, and it takes many lifetimes'. Indeed, when Andy followed up Nora's last comment by asking if this is what we call karma, she replied: 'That is the word chosen down there, but here it is just called a lesson.'

Meanwhile Claire and Amy were a little more forthcoming on the same theme:

> To experience as many emotions and realities as possible... To experience all that is and can be. Different experiences help to make the soul feel whole again before it returns to the Source.

> To help your own soul to grow, as an individual entity. Your soul is made up of all the experiences, all the challenges, all the strengths you've gained in overcoming things. Although it feels interminable actually doing it, from the spirit world being full of those learnings and experiences has created who you are. You become more sure of your place in the scheme of things.

As something of a follow-up to our discussion of light and dark in section 1.9, Alva, Veronica and Katrine also added some perspective to this question by implying that the convention karmic model of 'positive' and 'negative' or 'good' and 'bad', and of karmic 'rules' or 'laws', is a nonsense:

> We must follow our path. There is no right, there is no wrong, there is only experience... We are sent out to grow, to experience, in all facets of all different forms, in all different levels.

> Because all souls are part of the universal Source, rather than any rules or laws there is a 'way of being' that is followed... There is an inbuilt honor and respect that governs all actions, because all are working towards the plan... Free will is supreme on the physical plane, but all choices eventually lead towards the highest good.

> We don't have any rules or laws. We live with an understanding that everybody can do what they like because of free will... But underneath it all we understand each other, we all know what we have to do for the whole.

Of course, as Veronica suggests, the ultimate objective must be that of the Source itself. Despite this being an issue that Michael Newton and the other pioneers do not discuss, we will shortly find that a number of our sources provided views about this that were not only consistent with each other, but also with this issue of our objectives as individual souls.

But before we move on, it is worth taking a moment to step back and consider what all this means. For millennia, most religions – and certainly those that still dominate in the West – have relied on laying down moral codes and guidelines to their followers. The fact that these are subjective and differ from religion to religion is not hard to appreciate in the modern world, with its massive culture clashes. But what the modern evidence tells us is that there is *no* strict moral code or set of laws and obligations that can be laid down, certainly not from a truly spiritual perspective.

Of course that is not to say that we do not need laws and guidelines from a cultural perspective to attempt to ensure that as human beings we rub along with each other as best we can. But ultimately it is not for any one person to tell another what they should and should not do or think, especially not from any supposedly moral perspective. It tends to be the case that even the slightest attempt to adopt a soul perspective completely removes the kind of moral certainty and indignation with which our human perspective normally feels so secure. So the only thing that matters ultimately is to take *personal responsibility* for our own choices – and even if we fail to do this while incarnate, all truths will be laid bare when we return to the light and regain our soul perspective.

2.1.1 Can some souls choose not to reincarnate?

This related question is not often asked, and before we consider it we should examine a little more closely exactly what we mean by reincarnation. We all understand what it means for a soul to reincarnate on planet earth as a human being. As we have seen it commences with the nonphysical soul joining with the body of the baby in the womb, then eventually returning to the light when that physical body dies. This cycle carries on until the soul has gained all the experience of the physical plane that it needs, and has nothing left to learn there – although as we will see in section 2.5 it will then continue growing in the light realms or in other dimensions.

We can also imagine that a similar process would be involved if a soul decided to incarnate as another sort of lifeform on another physical planet, whether or not they ever experienced life on earth. But the pioneers' regression evidence also suggests that other less physical planets exist in other dimensions. It seems that it is possible for souls to genuinely reincarnate on such planets, even if the exact process is rather more difficult to envisage. To complete the options, it also seems that it is possible for souls to merely *visit* the astral plane of a physical planet, or to merely *experience* other less physical planets, without incarnating there. We will return to these various possibilities in section 2.6.

Taking all this into account, our sources were unanimous that virtually all souls *choose* to experience a cycle of genuine reincarnation in some sort of physical or semi-physical environment as part of their development. Here are Amy, Alva, Naomi and Veronica:

> You do choose to reincarnate, and you can choose to do it in other places... Other dimensions, other frequencies, other life experiences. This is only one of them... But they all involve learning experiences. That's the whole purpose of our existence.

> It does not happen very often. The soul will always have a longing and a yearning to grow.

> There is a community of souls who choose not to reincarnate and we don't condemn them for it, that is the pace they want to go at. They do have a slow rate of growth, but that is alright with them and it is alright with us.

> At spirit level, reincarnation is one of the most profoundly exciting developmental events, and to do it is not a chore. It is hard in some lives, but that's looking through it with physical eyes. Those who do not reincarnate are working towards developing in a different way... Understanding can be achieved through knowing physical trauma, but other people may have that understanding immediately without having to undergo any trauma. All choose the path of development that is right for them.

The general impression gained from this is that only rarely would a soul never experience reincarnation in some form or another, and that even then other options would be available for learning and growth – even if they were somewhat more restricted and involved slower progress. However Denise was adamant that 'all souls need to reincarnate at some point, without it their experience would be incomplete', and she was apparently backed up by Nora:

> They wouldn't learn then, but they can choose to take a break. Then they are encouraged to come back and, even though it's hard, we all want to learn.

Meanwhile Claire and Nadine emphasized the extent to which emotional lessons can be learned far better in the physical than the light plane – although we will return to the issue of whether the specific *earth* experience is unique in section 2.6:

> It's a choice whether to incarnate and to experience all the emotions. Some choose not to... They choose other planes of existence, in other realities, other realms, which are not necessarily physical. Reincarnation

on earth is just one of many experiments, but it involves a range of emotions that it is just not possible to experience on the spirit plane. So it's a brave experience.

You don't have to reincarnate on earth if you don't want to, although somehow you feel compelled to. But there comes a point where a soul may feel that they have learned all they need to on earth, and can move onto other planes, to learn new things... There are many things souls can do on the spiritual plane to learn too... It depends on what you want to learn. If you're perhaps working on emotional or physical lessons, then the earth plane is the easiest and quickest way because matter is so heavy. If you're working on things of a higher nature, like lessons of pure connection, of creation, of manifestation on an energetic rather than on a physical level, then this is easier on the spiritual plane.

2.1.2 Can you comment on the suggestion that the reincarnation cycle is just an illusion, and that when this is recognized a soul can return to the Source?

Early in the Introduction I referred to the view held by a number of modern spiritual commentators – usually influenced by traditional Buddhist, Gnostic and mystical thought, combined with modern scientific and psychedelic research – that the reincarnation cycle, and even the notion that we are individual souls, is an illusion. Let us now explore this view in rather more detail.

We cannot discuss Buddhism, even briefly, without understanding a little about the Hinduism from which it sprang. Traditionally Hindus accept the idea that the soul reincarnates as an individual entity. But they see karma primarily as a law of action and reaction, in which human souls can at least be demoted to a lower caste or even to animal lives as a punishment for bad karma. So those who are most committed will attempt to break free from the cycle of reincarnation completely by generating *no* further karma *at all*, whether good or bad – thereby allowing themselves to rejoin the Ultimate Source. It is from this idea that the principle of 'non-attachment' derives, and it is practiced by ascetics who completely remove themselves from any sort of dependence on both people and things, and spend the bulk of their time in meditation. Generally speaking we should have no doubt that there is much to be gained from keeping a sense of detachment and balanced impassivity in the face of our inevitable successes and failures. Having said that, it is worth remembering that in the *Bhagavad Gita* Krishna himself makes it clear that asceticism is not necessarily the answer, and that only full engagement in the physical world can produce real enlightenment.

Turning now to Buddhism itself, although it has many strains one of its central tenets is the concept of *anatta* or 'no self'. This is an often misunderstood idea – perhaps not surprisingly – but in highly simplistic terms it suggests that we are not individually reincarnating souls at all. It accepts that any karmic charge a person creates in one life does transfer into another body, but maintains that there is no continuity of personality or individuality between those two lives. Non-attachment is also central to Buddhism, but in this case not so that the individual generates no more karma but because the very notion of individuality itself is an illusion, or *maya*. So the only idea that matters is to recognize that we are all One.

Although there is no obvious, direct link between the two, there are some parallels between such Far Eastern mysticism and the Hermetic and Gnostic texts of the Near East. The latter in particular tend to offer a somewhat bleak, dehumanized view of the entire physical world as an abomination created by a fallen angel who thought that he could challenge God's supremacy. Indeed, for some this whole illusory schema of individually reincarnating souls, and even of light and physical planes, is maintained by some sort of conspiratorial cabal of fallen, dark entities. But the message is essentially the same: recognize the illusion of individuality and one is immediately released from bondage, and can adopt the natural or default state of rejoining the Source.

Let there be no doubt that the fundamental idea that we are all part of one Ultimate Source has justifiably widespread support. Not only is the experience of Oneness or the 'unity of everything' central to most psychedelic and other transcendental and enlightenment experiences, but it is backed up by modern scientific research into the holographic nature of the universe. Nevertheless, it is surely a fundamental mistake to take this to the further extreme of suggesting that all sense of individuality is mere illusion. It goes completely against the various strands of modern evidence we have reviewed so far in this book, including the evidence for individual soul reincarnation from regression and children who remember past lives, and the abundant evidence for the survival of the individual 'soul personality' provided by interlife regression research. We will return to how the general ideas of soul unity and individuality can be reconciled shortly.

In any case, we have already seen that our sources are unanimous that the purpose of reincarnation is for individual souls to learn and grow by experience. This is clearly fundamentally opposed to the idea that any soul can break free from the cycle at any point, merely by recognizing the illusion of individuality. These two views *cannot* be reconciled, and are mutually exclusive. And what we might refer to as the 'unity worldview' seems to be gaining in popularity in some circles at least. So we deliberately asked our sources whether such 'escape from the illusion' is possible.

Amy was short and to the point when she replied simply 'that's not feasible'. Alva, Katrine, Denise and Naomi were equally dismissive:

> That is *their* illusion... They have chosen, and they know within their energy, that they have come to earth to experience.

> That is part of their learning process... Although as you become closer to the One you reach a stage where you don't have to reincarnate any more because you have learned.

> That decision is made in the spirit realms, in conjunction with other souls... It is *not* made on the earth plane.

> You can't reduce the lessons into one life. But if you were able to karmically work through everything in a very short time, then that would reduce the number of lives that you had to have.

On a somewhat different tack, in the earliest sessions Andy was asking a slightly less specific question about whether there are any special spiritual practices that aid soul development. Although they therefore come from a slightly different angle, David and Veronica's answers were highly enlightening:

> Following a spiritual practice on earth is a good tool for development, but none of them are the truth, none of them have the whole picture. The fragments they all have are valuable… But on earth there are distortions, and more dead-end paths than free paths – which can mean people get stuck and get smaller, rather than growing.

> There are many different ways of developing, and while a high level of spiritual enlightenment can be achieved through years of meditation, the same level can be achieved in a fraction of a second through laughter… Some practice spiritual development through meditation and seeking enlightenment, or through prayer and worship, while others do it through experiencing the other sides of life. Each is just as valid, and each has its own developmental purpose.

2.1.3 Why does the Source manifest into all the forms in the universe in the first place?

The real test of the unity worldview is to stand right back and ask this 'ultimate' question, which few dare to pose. Of course, some would suggest that we should not be so assumptive as to dare to investigate the ineffable motives of the ultimate deity itself. But even if we accept that any answer we arrive at might only be an approximation of a far more complex truth that our human brains simply could not understand, surely educated guesses are far better than avoidance, obfuscation or wild stabs in the dark? More specifically, it is surely reasonable to enquire as to what would be the point of the Source manifesting all the various forms in the universe in the first place, if its default position is one of perfection and unity?

So what did our sources make of this? Naomi alone appeared to be somewhat blocked when she answered 'I don't think it's helpful to know the answer – one needs to grow in spirit, and not analyze everything'. But a number of our other sources seemed to have no problem in confirming my own suspicions with a simple yet philosophically coherent answer that was entirely consistent with their previous comments about the purpose of reincarnation. Here are Alva, Amy and Denise:

> It's this longing for balance, experience and growth.

> Because of an overall desire to know and touch everything, to go to the limits of absolutely everything imaginable. It's all just infinite possibilities, infinite permutations.

> To remain vibrant and strong. By growing through diverse creations, the consciousness expands.

Meanwhile, when Andy asked Claire whether individual soul growth contributes to any growth in the Source she replied 'yes, there is a sense of movement and expansion'.

The Holographic Soul

To bring all of this together, it seems clear that the apparent misconceptions in many spiritual approaches – especially those that are influenced by a combination of Buddhist, Gnostic, psychedelic and modern scientific thought – stem from a desire to emphasize the idea of soul unity at all costs. Yet, as I pointed out tentatively in *The Book of the Soul*, there need be no dichotomy between unity and individuality. The full solution to this apparent paradox that I have since arrived at is extremely simple, and yet seems to have hitherto been overlooked. So let me state it formally:

- Soul consciousness is holographic. We are both individual

aspects of the Source, and full holographic representations of it, all at the same time. However this does *not* mean that soul individuality is in itself an illusion. The definition of a hologram is that the part *contains* the whole, and yet at the same time is clearly *distinguishable from* it.

- The Source's primary aim, in diversifying into all the billions of holographic soul aspects of itself that operate in the various realms throughout the universe, is to experience all that is and can be. As individualized aspects of the Source who have chosen to reincarnate on this planet, we are merely fulfilling a small part of that objective by gaining a balance of all the experiences available via this route.

In passing, a number of our sources seemed to confirm this crucial idea. In fact Naomi described this holographic duality perfectly: 'It's a paradox. Souls always have a sense of individuality and a sense of oneness all at the same time.' Both Amy and Alva seemed to be echoing these sentiments when they reported:

The Source is All. Everything in existence. All consciousness. It's as if we are all part of that body, as if we are universes within it.

It's like a big wheel with different compartments, spreading out from the Unity, the One. It separates so that it can experience all the different compartments, and then, when the experience is complete, bring it all back to the centre of itself.

The idea of the Holographic Soul has massive and widespread implications for our understanding of why we are here and how everything fits together. But more specifically it also clarifies two common misconceptions. The first is that it is a mistake to think of the reincarnation cycle on the physical plane as something to be 'escaped from', because it is an essential and invaluable experience both on an individual and a unified level. The second is that in some senses it is equally mistaken to talk about 'reuniting with the Source', because we are already, and have always been, fundamentally united with it. The only context in which such an idea would make sense would be if the Source did periodically reabsorb all or some of its individualized soul aspects back into itself, as Alva seems to suggest above, and we will return to this possibility in section 2.3.

In terms of other related attempts to apply the idea of the hologram, Newton uses it to describe how the soul 'splits' its energy and only brings a proportion back into incarnation, but this is perfectly compatible with my new, broader definition. Indeed, the various ways in which soul energy can fragment, which we discussed in sections 1.1 to 1.4, also make far more sense if we think of it as holographic. By contrast, scientific postulations of a 'holographic universe' have been precisely what has led their proponents to the conclusion that all notions of individuality are illusory, but this fails to take account of the entirety of the evidence from both sides of the coin. So to link the idea of the hologram to soul energy itself in the broadest sense is arguably its ultimate and proper application.

Human versus Animal Souls

2.2 Are there differences between human and animal soul energy?

The next issue that presents itself when we are considering the subject of soul development is whether there is a distinction between human and other souls. So far we have talked entirely within a human soul context. But a number of reincarnatory religions suggest that souls develop in the physical plane by evolving through the ranks of mineral, vegetable and animal life before attaining human status. Furthermore, Hinduism in particular holds that we can be punished by devolution back down the ranks and having to start again.

I certainly accept the idea that every lifeform has some sort of underlying soul consciousness, precisely because everything is a holographic aspect of the Source. I also accept that all soul energy originally comes from this same Source. But are there differences in how various types of soul consciousness operate and contribute to the experience of the whole?

A number of the pioneers cite evidence suggesting that animal soul energy is more collective than individualized, and this idea is supported by Newton's reports that human souls are created especially for that purpose. Our sources were unanimous that there are indeed differences. Naomi merely indicated that 'animal energy is not the same, although they have souls'; Nora that 'animal souls are in another group, they are not included in the same system'; and Claire that 'they have a different frequency, amplitude, density or tuning'. But, despite the differences, Nadine, Alva, Veronica and Denise were at pains to remind us that all soul energy comes from the one Ultimate Source:

They are separate... There is an infinite amount of consciousness for different types of awareness, and humans are only one aspect of it.

There's one wheel for humans, another one for animals, and another one for minerals, and so on, but they all come from the same Source.

Animals and humans are all part of the same soul energy, which chooses what form it wants to incarnate into.

They have different frequencies... It starts with a spark that can flicker many ways. Animal soul energy chooses to work with instinct and innocence as the driving force. The human choice is more complicated and difficult because of a higher level of consciousness and free will. The creative energy source takes on the chosen differences.

Several of our sources also confirmed the idea of animal soul energy being more collective. Here are Veronica, again, and Katrine:

In animal form there is a shared energy, a link, and they do not need to speak or organize because they share a knowing about when it's time to migrate, when it's time to run, and so on.

Animals are bred more as a group energy, although different kinds of animals have their own group. Each member of the group has the same soul energy, but they have a group power.

Let us now turn to the issue of whether animal souls also evolve and grow, whether by reincarnation or some other mechanism. Amy suggested that they do not:

Animal energy is more elemental, they tend to have a less reasoning, rational mind, and less ability to solve problems. They're considered to be companion souls, but they are part of the elemental kingdom, they are not part of soul evolution... They are creations, they are not expected to evolve in the same way as a human... They are more connected to trees and plants. All of these have a consciousness of their own, but animals are more intuitively connected... Human souls are born with a purpose, but animal souls don't have that, they are created to be connected to the elemental rather than human kingdom.

However I am intuitively inclined to side more with Nora and David, who insisted that animal soul energy does evolve, even if on a different path to that of humans:

Animal souls do progress into more complex animal forms, so they evolve as well. And smarter animal souls, such as monkeys and dolphins, can teach us quite a lot.

They have different qualities. We are all part of the same energy, but with animal souls it's a much simpler, straightforward kind... In a beehive, each bee has a fraction of that energy and the hive as a whole has another fraction... Animal soul energy can develop within itself in the same way that a human soul develops and grows. It's not that it has further to go, it's just on a different path... It's about allowing each fragment to express itself fully as an individual, and allowing it to take the path that it needs to. At this stage that is the goal, to give all these fragments full expression of what they are. Only from that place of full understanding and full expression can we start the path back to the One.

With hindsight it might have been interesting if we had asked our sources if animal souls actually reincarnate, because this is not something I have seen discussed before. However my best guess would be that reports of them having somewhat more collectivized soul energy would preclude this possibility, and require some other mechanism to link their soul energy to the physical. But this is an obvious potential area for further research.

It is somewhat unfortunate that the idea that human and animal souls are not the same is sometimes taken to be elitist – and even a throwback to the Christian dogma that insisted that the earth was at the centre of the universe, giving humankind a position of unique importance. From my own perspective nothing could be further from the truth, especially when we factor in the fact that earth is unlikely to be unique in harboring reasonably sophisticated lifeforms. Our sources also repeatedly emphasized the need for humanity to return to a position of respect for and balance with our environment and planet, so that all lifeforms work together as part of the great Unity. Although we will examine this issue in far more detail in section 3.4, here is a foretaste from Alva:

A lot of animals are now feeling what humans call the stressed environment. They have always been very much in contact with the energy from the earth, but now they're experiencing the unbalancing... This is between the three kingdoms of animals, humans and the earth. They all need to find the same vibration... To move into the balancing point together by being united in their oneness as energies. But because humans have the ability to make choices, they need to be leading the process... Animals can only react.

2.2.1 Can human souls develop from animal souls?

Needless to say, the differences in soul energy themselves suggest that it would be impossible for an animal soul to develop into a human one, as Hindus for example suggest. But we nevertheless asked our sources to comment on this issue. Amy and Denise both said it was not possible, while Katrine and Nora proffered 'although all souls are created from the same material, nobody *comes from* an animal soul' and 'although their energy is similar, it is not interchangeable' respectively. Alva, Claire and Naomi also rejected the possibility but, accompanied by Katrine, emphasized that in the light realms a human soul would be able to link to any type of animal soul energy – or at least experience – in order to gain an understanding of the nature of its existence. This would not be dissimilar to the ideas of projection or sharing soul memories that were discussed in section 1.6.

These reports seem to be somewhat at odds with the findings of a few regression pioneers, most notably Morris Netherton and Hans TenDam, a few of whose subjects were regressed back before their first human incarnation and seemed to experience animal lives. However we cannot be sure that these represented true incarnations of that individual soul, rather than mere projections. So it may be that human souls can choose to tap into animal soul experiences, and it may be that the latter are more generally recycled through to human beings via the Source, as we will discover in the next section. But I would still maintain that there is no mechanism by which an individual animal soul could progress into a human one and maintain continuity of identity and so on.

Despite its connotations of karmic punishment that are completely at odds with a dynamic of learning and experience, and despite the differences in soul energy, Andy did incidentally ask several of our sources to comment on the Hindu notion that human souls can *devolve* back down the ranks. As expected David gave a flat 'no', while Katrine reported that 'once a soul is human it stays that way – it would be a big step backwards'.

Soul Birthing and the Recycling of Experience

Note that David and Claire were not asked any of these questions.

2.3 How are new souls created?

Having established the background understanding that reincarnation is a cycle of learning, growth and experience, that the Source itself manifests in order to grow and experience, and that different types of souls are created for different purposes and to experience different forms, our next question takes us back to the beginning of the soul's journey – its point of creation. This is something that Newton in particular discusses in some depth. Here are Nadine, Alva and Naomi:

> It's like the form is pushed out. It's like there is a massive big ball of cotton candy, and inside it there is an energy that's pushing outwards. And, with that, the little bits of cotton candy come off.

> There are special souls that nurture new souls after they have been born from the Source... They surround them with a small ball of light so the energy can grow stronger, to sort of hold it in place.

> You have specialist teams who cleave off part of the Source energy to create a new fledgling soul... They carve off what is required, that is their specialist decision... It depends on the path of the soul and its purpose. Each soul would already have a purpose... Each soul will be created for a function, with a specialist purpose that is part of the bigger whole... The Source knows about this, and the soul itself will learn what its purpose is over time. It will find it has core skills and traits and naturally go in that direction.

But it was Amy who provided the most complete description of the birth and nurturing of a new soul, which is worth providing in full:

> The new soul emerges out of a white light, a little bit like an egg being released from the ovary. It comes out empty and yet full of potential. And there are like specialist souls who help it, because it is like a newborn baby.
> *Can you talk a little bit about the role of these specialist souls, and how they work?*
> They are like midwives, who nurture all the new souls in a special environment because their energy is so raw, so open and pure – but only because it has not been formed, or gained any of the experiences that will give it its identity and individuality. And they have to reach a certain point before they can take their first step into the physical plane.
> *Just tell me a little bit about what happens before this first step.*
> It's like sending a toddler to school, you don't send them too early. They have to get used to being a soul to begin with, to learn about the world of spirit, so it's quite gentle, everything's very soft and slow. A lot of love is projected to them, which is the first thing they ever feel. The energies of the souls who nurture them are incredibly gentle.
> *Do they have any life experiences at an energy level before they incarnate in the physical?*
> They have the experience of being with their groups. They see it as being with their family. They've grown with these souls, so the groups can be very large.
> *Do they receive any teachings or anything like that in the spirit realms?*
> Yes. They have to be prepared for their first lifetime. They're not thrown

in at the deep end and given a really hard lifetime, because they have to learn about how much energy they need to take, and that can be quite scary.

What sort of very first life would they have?

They might choose a quite privileged lifetime where they don't have to work too hard, just to have the experience of being in a physical body, because it's hard enough just to understand and learn and come to terms with having a body. It's such a vastly different experience to anything they've had on the spiritual levels that it has to be very gentle. Or some might choose just to be a baby for a little while, spending a couple of years and then leaving. It takes time to get used to having a body. It takes a lot of lifetimes to learn about the interplay between a soul and a body. And they have to be taught all the way along, so they're very closely guided.

What sort of help and support do they receive?

Initially they tend to be put in more family-oriented or community-based environments. Their guides can also incarnate to keep an eye on them... Usually as an older relation or friend, which gives them a feeling of familiarity, even if they're not consciously aware of what the connection is.

Finally Veronica, unusually, seemed to be somewhat overwhelmed by this question. But I include her response because it does appear to confirm the idea of the Holographic Soul:

I'm sorry, I've got so much, it's hard to verbalize. Souls are part of the infinite energy. We think of them as souls, as separate entities, as separate things who choose to incarnate in different forms, but they are all part of the universal energy. The energy that 'is', the energy of Source. There are just different facets to that energy that are what we call souls. Therefore a new soul is only new because it is an energy that's given a purpose.

2.3.1 At some point will the Source draw all soul energy back into itself, and then start the whole process of creation again in an endless cycle?

The Hindu concept of 'Days and Nights of Brahma' is reasonably well-known. But, as I explained at some length in my second book, *Genesis Unveiled*, the idea that the earth and its inhabitants are regularly destroyed and recreated in 'world cycles' is not easily reconciled with geological, archaeological, evolutionary and general scientific evidence. However the broader idea is that there are endless and lengthy 'universal cycles' – more accurately associated with 'Lives of Brahma' – in which the Source periodically manifests itself into all the forms in the universe before reabsorbing everything back into itself. This is a far more philosophically and scientifically reasonable idea. Indeed I have always referred to the Big Bang as 'just another dawn of Brahma'.

It was not until after I had completed *The Book of the Soul* that I began to concentrate on the ultimate question, and came to realize that the main aim of the Source is to experience. As a result I intuitively suggested that the experience gained by all the various forms in all the various planes would only be properly reintegrated with the Source at each point of reabsorption in the endless cycle. I also suggested that perhaps this collective experience would be used as a new starting point and frame of reference for the next round of manifestation. But I have never previously written about this mystery of how the Source might recycle the experience of all its aspects, and nor, as far as I am aware, has anyone else.

The responses to this question therefore came as one of the biggest shocks to emerge from our research. Indeed it is this set of answers, combined with one or two others that we will come to in due course, that convinces us of the legitimacy of our research, and of the wisdom and enlightenment that can surely only have come from our subjects' ethereal sources themselves. Because not only did a number of them choose to concentrate on the issue of how experience is recycled through the Source, but in doing so they provided a consistent and insightful solution to a mystery that our subjects subsequently confirmed they had never consciously contemplated. Not only that, but the information they came up with was completely new to *us*, and not what we had anticipated at all. However on reflection it makes perfect sense, especially when one properly considers the implications of my own proposal that we are all merely holographic representations of the Source at all times.

What they revealed is that the Source is *constantly recycling* the experience gained by all its aspects. Nadine opened the issue up in our very first session by revealing that 'the Source is constantly releasing new souls, and constantly bringing back in'. Andy picked up on this and asked her what it was drawing back into itself, to which she replied 'an enfoldment of awareness'. Under further questioning she then confirmed that this was the awareness of all the souls already in existence. Amy corroborated this view, indicating that 'because of the way in which new souls are created from the Source there is a circular pattern'. Moreover, with further questioning she too confirmed that whenever new souls are created their energy effectively contains the up-to-date experience of the Source, so there is a 'constant recycling'. More of the same came from Denise, who reported that 'the Source is a point of absolute remembrance that doesn't stay the same, but is constantly changing and moving and expanding'. She also indicated separately that, as a result, 'human souls have the experience of animal souls within them'. Meanwhile Nora was the only one of our sources who was prompted on this issue by Andy, because of the results of earlier sessions. But she agreed that newly created souls have more experience and knowledge now than they would have done previously 'because the whole thing has evolved since the beginning – so although they still have to learn the lessons, some can now be learned faster than before'.

However this time it was Alva who waxed most lyrical about the whole topic of recycling experience, although this only came up incidentally when Andy was asking her why new souls need to be created:

> There always needs to be a circulation.
> *Does this lead to any problems on earth?*
> Do they know they are old or new souls? In their conscious mind, they don't know much about it.
> *But would younger souls be more likely to have problems?*
> We think of a new soul as being sort of primitive, and less developed. But they don't have to be if they're coming from the Oneness… They can be sent down with a lot more experience from this new energy… That is the way to obtain balance between old and new souls, so there doesn't have to be a difference between them.

Some critics have suggested that to talk of some souls being more 'advanced' than others is elitist and divisive. Indeed I am sufficiently in agreement with this that I now prefer to use the word *experienced*. However it does seem to be an inescapable fact that some souls are further into their karmic journey than others. Nevertheless, we should never attempt to guess at our own level of soul experience while in incarnation because we cannot know this with any sort of certainty – and certainly the type of life we have is no indicator because the most experienced souls can choose the most apparently difficult and impoverished lives deliberately. Moreover, Alva's crucial new perspective on this issue is that, although a younger soul may have less individual experience, they balance this by having more collective experience in their soul energy make-up. So for this reason alone they should not be regarded as in any way inferior. Ultimately we are not in a race that can be 'won' by high-performing individual souls, as Naomi pointed out:

All souls are different and they all progress at a different rate... Every soul is growing towards perfection, and they can choose to follow that path slowly, quickly or stand still.

So we should recognize that we are all in this collective experience together, and the best we can do is not only further our own growth, but use our best endeavors to assist that of others as well. Progressive, altruistic behavior helps everyone to move forwards.

Reuniting with the Source

There is a new possibility that arises from the idea that all souls are holographic aspects of the Source itself, which is that the experience of individual souls might be automatically and continuously recycled back into the Source without there being any need for them to 'reunite' with it in any formal sense. Nevertheless Amy was insistent that 'the aim is still to merge back with the Source'. So it seems that all souls move towards a point where they do eventually reunite.

However, given the fluidity and choice that seems to govern everything, it would be no surprise if this was a somewhat individual process with no set rules as to what has to be 'achieved' for remerger to occur. Indeed, in the next section we will encounter the idea that damaged souls sometimes reunite with the Source before they have even completed the earthly reincarnation cycle, let alone gone through the far more extensive potential development in the light and other realms that usually follows. Nevertheless, the rider on this is that it seems most souls would actively want to pursue all avenues laid out in their 'soul plan'. That is, not only the various aspects of general emotional experience common to all souls who reincarnate on earth, but also the particular specialisms that can be developed in various realms that each soul seems to have as a specific purpose from the moment of its creation. So it would seem that to reunite before one's own soul plan is fully carried through would be perfectly possible, but unusual – and it is certainly not our primary aim during the reincarnation cycle, as those who support a unity worldview would suggest.

However much individual souls may have the option to make their own choices about reuniting with the Source, Alva was unique in making the suggestion that most do so in *groups* who are all 'in balance':

It seems like there are large groupings of souls that go gradually towards the Oneness. And each and every soul in each grouping needs to have the right experience so that they will all be in balance. And they will merge with other groupings, and they will go further until they are all in balance. Then they all go into the Source as one balanced energy.

This idea is remarkably similar to one presented by the mid-twentieth century Qabalist Dion Fortune, who is one of the very few people whose channeled material, although highly esoteric, seems broadly sensible. She discusses the idea of groups of souls or 'monads' operating in cycles, the only difference being that she tends to relate such activity to each 'logos' or solar system, each of which is a Source within the Ultimate Source.

Our sources were so keen to concentrate on the issue of the continuous recycling of knowledge that the original question of whether or not the Hindu concept of universal cycles remains valid was left largely unanswered. It is certainly not essential if experience is *constantly* recycled, even if this does involve souls formally reuniting with the Source individually or in groups. So is there any practical need for the Source to periodically reabsorb everything back into itself all in one go? Apparently not according to Katrine, who was one of only two of our sources who answered this question directly:

> The Source does not start again from scratch, because the process is infinite, and the learnings will always be there... New souls are created all the time. And there will never be a time when all souls have completed all learnings.

She accompanied her suggestion that this is a continuous process that will never be completed by indicating that, rather than collapsing back in on itself, the universe will continue to expand – which is, of course, what some modern cosmologists are now suggesting. However Naomi seemed to side with those cosmologists in the cyclical camp:

> The big bang that created the universe is not when time started. It happens again and again.

Given that modern science is just as split as these two sources, it seems only sensible that we should reserve judgment as to whether or not the Hindu proposition of universal cycles is just as mistaken as that of lesser world cycles. But we should also remember that, as we will see in section 4.2, the concept of time itself probably has little relevance in the grand scheme of things. Indeed this may be the factor that makes our attempts to understand this issue from a human perspective somewhat confusing and inadequate.

Development During the Reincarnation Cycle

2.4 Do all souls have a full interlife experience every time?

In section 1.7 we encountered the idea that less experienced souls may accept less guidance and help in the light realms, and may as a result return to incarnation swiftly without proper healing or review of past-life traumas, or proper planning of their next life. I also suggested that this might tend to lead to repetitive karmic patterns.

Our sources were especially loquacious on this topic, and we will find shortly that they did provide some support for the suggestion that less experienced souls might have a curtailed interlife experience. However in the first instance they indicated that there are other reasons as well. To start us off, Veronica provided the following general assessment that not all souls need to experience every aspect during every interlife:

> There is always a process to be gone through, but only what is needed takes place. It may not be necessary to meet with other souls that were in incarnation, or to look over all of the events of the life. It may be that the healing and development between lives is so automatic that it occurs just by going through the different energies of the spirit realm.

Meanwhile Nadine emphasized that if a soul agreed to an altruistic life where the lessons were not primarily for them, they too might not have such a full experience. Claire agreed with this, providing a detailed description of how such a soul might return to the same environment quickly after a short first life to help the family deal with that first loss, in which case both lives would have been planned in advance:

> A soul who agrees to take the body of a baby who dies at a very young age can reincarnate again very quickly, and it would have been agreed beforehand... So if the first life is to teach other souls a life lesson, then the second life may be agreed at the same time... When babies die very young the soul can reincarnate in the same family, or nearby. Because the lesson of the first, short life is for the parents, the soul may reincarnate as another relative of the same family, to be in the same environment to continue helping the parents with their life's lesson. It's not a lesson for themselves but for others.

She added that a swift return might also be made if a soul 'needed to be in a similar timeframe for a particular lesson, or with particular souls who were already incarnated'.

Our sources also made observations about general differences in the interlife experiences of younger and older souls. Claire emphasized the greater variety of interlife options available to the latter:

> More experienced souls may not need so much guidance, because they have more wisdom and know better what's possible and what experiences will be best for them before they reincarnate. But there are more choices and alternatives for them in the spirit realms, so they may choose to stay longer.

Veronica made the interesting point that, while any soul can have a traumatic life, more experienced souls need longer to assimilate their consequences and lessons because only they deliberately *choose* such lives:

> Older, more established souls tend to be the ones who experience the denser, more traumatic lives, so they tend to take more time to understand these lives. Younger souls may not have chosen lives in that way, so will not have as much to heal and assimilate in the spirit realms.

Naomi, as well as agreeing that 'the interlife is longer if you've had a hard life, when you've had more to absorb and deal with', tended to see the receiving or giving of teaching as the major differentiator between younger and older souls:

> Although younger souls have a more playful time in the interlife, there is perhaps more teaching when you are younger. More advanced souls tend to act *as* teachers.

Finally Nora concentrated more on the earliest lives of younger souls:

> Younger souls don't tend to do so much work up here. The first few times there are so many lessons to be learned on earth that there is not much time needed in between.

Damaged, Disoriented and Impetuous Souls

Let us now turn to certain specific problems that apparently less experienced souls can face. The first concerns Newton's reports that some are so damaged that they may have to be 'reshaped' or even 'remodeled' via infusions of new soul energy. We have also seen Alva's similar report about severely damaged trapped souls in section 1.1. However Naomi described an even more drastic treatment, and it is this report that I referenced in the previous section when discussing how damaged souls can reunite with the Source early and individually:

> Some souls decide they don't want to return, while for some *we* decide

that they don't return... We sit down with each of them and discuss what path they should follow. Some may go to other dimensions that are easier – or not so much easier but have experiences that can benefit that soul. Other souls will go to another place for recuperation, and they will stay there and grow in a different way. All souls will grow and be reunited, but also some souls will be changed... Some souls can be too damaged and then we can't let them continue reincarnating, so they are best described as reuniting with the Source at an earlier stage, even though they haven't learned everything. They are made into new souls to go out again. I suppose it's a death and a rebirth in a different way, but this is something they are happy to agree to.

The second problem concerns souls that do leave earth's astral plane but do not make the full transition into the light realms, because they remain so disoriented and confused that they refuse to accept any sort of healing. Denise specifically reported on this aspect, and repeatedly referred to souls – including some who have committed suicide – who remain stuck in what she calls the 'grey place':

> For some souls the desire to evolve is resisted, and they stay in the grey place. There are many chances, and no one is forgotten. But some souls don't learn, or have a stronger negative pull, and they wait in the grey place for help and guidance, or self-realization.
> *I thought all souls went through a healing process after death where negative thoughts are removed?*
> Some don't accept the healing. Some don't accept the death.
> *And are they known as earthbound souls?*
> They're not all earthbound. Some can be in spirit in the grey place with some negative energies attached, with fear and indecision even in spirit.

It is not entirely clear from Denise's account as to whether souls who remain stuck in the grey place can reincarnate from there without entering the light realms proper at all. However it seems this may be possible, and if so they would represent a more severe version of the third problem. This is when apparently impetuous younger souls do move through to the light realms proper, but either refuse the healing, review and planning guidance that is available to all, or choose to ignore it once given. As a result they have a somewhat curtailed and incomplete interlife experience.

In addition to giving pointers towards this behavior when discussing how traumatic body memories are carried over in section 1.7, a number of our sources commented on it here. Although brief, Amy reported that 'if a soul does not take a good enough break in between lives, it looses vital integration'. Nadine, Alva and Claire were somewhat more forthcoming, emphasizing that a sense of unfinished business is a major factor – just as it can be for spirits who remain stuck in the astral plane, as we saw in section 1.1:

> If somebody felt that they hadn't fulfilled all their intentions – and they felt that they were so close, they didn't want to stop, they were 'on a roll' – they would come back down very quickly without going through all the reviews that you would normally. But usually that doesn't happen, because souls feel that it's a rest to leave the earth plane and not come back so quickly.

> The majority of those who reincarnate swiftly are younger souls, especially those who have had very sudden and unexpected deaths... Some souls make a bad choice that leads to sudden departure.

> Some souls do choose to reincarnate quickly, without experiencing all there is to experience – before they should really, but it's their choice... They miss out on the guidance, which is not a good thing... Sometimes souls choose to reincarnate because they wish to return just to be near loved ones still on earth. Or perhaps they feel a need to complete their life's purpose quickly, and want to return to a similar timeframe and environment to finish things off... Once the necessary healing or energy work has been done they have a choice as to how quickly they reincarnate. There's always choice. Advice is given, but they can choose whether or not to accept it.

Later on Andy asked Claire to comment further on this issue, and she made a number of important observations – first that a soul might choose to reincarnate without even reuniting with its core soul energy, and second that they may avoid full healing and review precisely because they fear judgment from others:

> *When souls do not receive all their energy healing, is that by choice?*
> Less experienced souls can choose to return quickly without realizing they've missed out. That choice is always there for them.
> *What are the implications if a soul does not receive proper healing?*
> They would reincarnate with remnants of their past life, imprints on their energy body, negativities perhaps. And they may have missed a coming together with the energy they left behind, so they would return with kind of a stale energy. It's not a good thing.
> *Why would a soul choose not to have this energy healing?*
> They are attracted to life on earth, and they want to return to experience all those emotions as quickly as possible. Less experienced souls are not so wise, they have more to learn.

Does this happen very frequently?

No... Some souls who feel they have failed their lessons may want to repeat them, and feel that is the way to do it, but it's not that easy. They hope to avoid acknowledging their failure in some way, because they are young souls and they fear judgment. But there is no judgment. They judge *themselves*, and are not aware that that is the only judgment they are going to meet.

So what experience would a soul who had no healing have between lives?

There is always some healing of energy, it's just a case of how much they choose to receive... Guidance would be offered for it to continue with the necessary energy changes, but there's always the choice to reject it.

When a new life is chosen for that soul, is their lack of healing taken into account?

Yes... It depends on what they need to learn, and whether they have sufficient energy remaining. If it is clear that they would be unable to undertake the same lesson by not having sufficient energy, then – it's never a rest – but it would be an easier life.

So they get help purely by the sort of life that is offered, even if they don't realize it?

Even if they choose not to accept guidance, it is always there. As they reincarnate it's like passing through a veil... But they can always receive more help once they've reincarnated when they're in their sleep state or in other states, because they are never alone.

It is interesting that David took this idea of fear of review a stage further, indicating that indoctrination by religion – from which it would naturally arise – is a major potential restriction on the experience:

Some younger souls mask themselves from it, because they are not ready to enter fully into the real world... This is because they are stuck with a great deal of fear from their life on earth, which they carry over – in particular those who have been indoctrinated into religions, and believe that it's going to be a certain way, so they get stuck in that experience. If their guides are not as advanced as they need to be it can be hard to pull them out from that... So after death they experience pretty much what they expect to experience. There are teams that work with them to help them to see the truth, but not always successfully. Sometimes they need to be allowed to experience another life completely to allow them to pull away.

All of this raises the additional question of how the lives of souls who reincarnate without properly experiencing the interlife are planned. As we might expect, Nora was adamant that 'their lives are more or less chosen for them'.

Planes, Levels and Aspects

In one part of the report above Claire specifically corroborated the idea I discussed in the Introduction that all souls must go through a healing and delayering process to enter the light realms proper – for example, to allow them to meet up with the other members of their soul group. But she also specifically hinted at the idea of different levels in the light plane:

> There has to be a rebalancing and recharging of energy before a soul is accepted by its soul group. It's necessary for the recognition process... Each frequency vibration occupies a plane or level, so souls on each level must have a similar frequency.

What is more, both Katrine and Denise confirmed this view:

> Souls have different experiences every time, they will not go to the same place, or meet the same people, they will do it differently each time... It would be boring to do the same thing all the time. Also they might progress to a different level because of what they've learned, so they don't have to go through all the stages any more – for example, they might just go straight to a briefing with the elders, whereas less experienced souls might have to undergo a lot of healing for various reasons... But every life has to be planned – less experienced souls may not be doing the planning themselves, but their lives are always planned.

> Some souls don't move through to the review and planning level. They stay on an initial level... For rest and rejuvenation... Usually this is because they are not ready to make choices... But when they are ready, they have new choices and options for learnings... There are layers in the spirit world, and also each soul will create what they believe to be there. Some stay on the level with spirit guides and helpers, and some choose different levels.

These reports clearly suggest that the interlife experience is varied and fluid, even if certain underlying elements can be identified. But they also shed further light on my basic model of the three planes – that is physical, astral and light. This represents something of an oversimplification, albeit a perfectly serviceable and helpful one for most discussions. But in *The Book of the Soul* I suggested that the astral probably contains different 'aspects', not least one for trapped human souls and another for so-called elementals and nature spirits. I also followed the lead of a number of pioneers in accepting that the light plane probably contains various levels – albeit that most attempts by more esoteric writers both ancient and modern to identify and describe the various levels and planes seem to be completely baffling, inconsistent and arguably unhelpful.

So what does this latest evidence tell us about the nature of the levels in the light plane? At the very least it appears that there is a 'transition level' in which healing and delayering occurs that operates as a link between the astral and light planes – and, according to Denise, some souls can remain in this transition level without receiving proper healing, in which case it is regarded as the grey place. It also seems likely that there is a 'guide and group' level in the light realms proper that is occupied by most reincarnating souls, and in which spirit guides and helpers are available to provide further assistance. But we might also expect there to be an 'elder level' in which these rather more experienced souls reside, and indeed further 'higher levels' beyond this that we cannot hope to describe and will only find out about when we too reach that stage of soul evolution. Not only that, but in each of these levels we might expect there to be different 'aspects' to which souls are attracted according to their level of experience and natural energy vibration.

I have tentatively attempted to represent this information in the diagram below in the hope of clarifying these ideas – which, we might note, do not conform closely to any schema put forward by Newton or any other researcher. Of course there are problems with putting such a framework together, because it can clearly only be an approximation that concentrates primarily on those areas relevant to reincarnating souls – which is what all interlife subjects are by definition. But we should be clear that those apparently enlightened souls who have supposedly provided details of the higher levels could only have done so if they were incarnating by choice to help the rest of us, rather than because they were still involved in the reincarnation cycle to gain experience. This is because almost certainly their true soul energy vibrations would have to be sufficiently high to allow them access to information about such levels. Moreover it is arguably unlikely that it would be useful for us to have such extended knowledge of levels that must increasingly approach the Source itself when we are, in general, so abjectly ignorant and misinformed about even the most basic framework. In addition, from a more general perspective we must be ever wary of allowing the concept of levels to introduce ideas of ego and elitism, remembering that such reactions are completely absent at a soul level – and that it is only in human form that we impose such unhelpful value judgments.

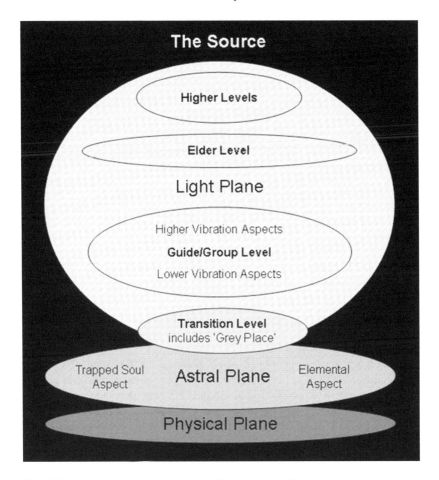

2.4.1 Why do some souls seem to display repetitive behavior over many lifetimes?

In the previous section our sources confirmed that younger and more impatient souls can return swiftly into incarnation without proper healing or planning, and therefore make decisions that are not in their own best interests. But we have already seen in the Introduction that there are certain basic emotional lessons that we all have to work through as part of our soul development. And the point that the majority of our sources reinforced here was that to a large extent repetitive behavior patterns are a perfectly natural by-product of this process. For example although, as we saw above, Alva admitted that some younger souls can make 'bad choices', she added a rider to this:

But especially when they are less experienced, they do not need that long in the spirit realms to regain their strength, and they really need to get back down there to face the same challenge again, but a little bit wiser.

Meanwhile Katrine too agreed with Andy's suggestion that souls who do not listen to the advice given to them are more likely to suffer from repetitive patterns, but she also added 'it's common for souls to go through the same situations – actually not situations, but *learnings*, over many lifetimes'. Nora agreed with this, although making something of a joke about those who tend to lag behind:

> We all have to work through all the lessons, and it takes some time. But some have been working on the same lessons again and again for a long time. We call them the 'slow ones'... If a soul had a lifetime where everything was planned to allow it to learn, but it came back and was like a naughty child that just didn't want to listen, it would be taken aside by the council and given a good talking-to. Then it would usually get it the next time or couple of times.

Amy provided more details along the same lines, comparing souls who are working through a particular lesson perfectly normally with those who actually get stuck on it and cannot seem to move forwards:

> As soon as they're incarnated, their planning is forgotten. The soul remembers, but they've forgotten, and that's part of the learning. It's only when you reach a certain point of development that your conscious awareness of the lesson or problem you are working on becomes useful. You've got to try and figure it out for yourself, and because other souls are in play in that dynamic it might not always be your fault – your lack of achievement might not necessarily be all down to you. So you're given a certain amount of time to learn the lesson. But if you've reached a point where you still can't quite manage it, then a little bit of help doesn't go amiss... So you might be given greater conscious knowledge and awareness so you can work to finally clear the issue... Souls that get *stuck* on a lesson tend to be less experienced. They become a little bit separate, they're not able to respond to the soul's promptings quite so easily, it all becomes too entrenched – and then they need help to break out of that pattern. But it's different when you are just working through them.

But undoubtedly the best description of the process of mastering basic emotional lessons was provided when Nora went into more detail:

> When soul groups are working together on a particular lesson they might have five lifetimes concentrating on just that, and they can change relationships between each other over those lives. They are pretty much planned in advance so that between them there is only a brief interlude,

although the gaps between them will gradually increase. Then, when they switch to a new lesson, there will be more work done in classrooms and so on, and the composition of the group may change a bit, or individuals might go and join a completely new group.

Are there standard areas of learning?

There are quite a few things that we all have to learn, such as to take responsibility, to be loved, to have power, to be a victim. All the emotions must be covered. So in one life, for example, we have to really use the emotion of anger and be in touch with it; then in another we have anger used *on us* by another soul. We need to experience the emotion from those different angles.

At what point does the soul know that it has mastered any given lesson?

Their council will discuss it with them, it's almost like a test to check where you are. But there is no point in pretending to be ready when you're not.

The conclusion we can draw from all this is that there is an important distinction to be made between two different types of repetitive behavior. On the one hand, less experienced souls can sometimes be in something of a hurry to return, and as a result fail to receive the full help and guidance available to them in the interlife. This will normally mean they have incomplete healing and review of strong 'unresolved' emotions, which they bring back with them but *not* by calculated choice. They also fail to be actively involved in the planning of their next life. This is likely to lead to what we might call a 'reactive pattern' of repetitive behavior that to some extent could have been avoided if they had made more informed decisions.

By contrast, it is also clear from our sources' comments here that souls can repeatedly work on the same emotional lesson even when they have received full healing and review, and are fully involved in the planning of their lives. Indeed we have already seen in the Introduction that souls deliberately select the 'in-progress' emotions they want to bring back into incarnation to work with again. All of this seems to represent the perfectly normal process by which all souls work on their basic emotional lessons. So these 'proactive' patterns of repetitive behavior are entirely different because they are characterized by informed choices.

To turn to more progressive soul choices for a moment, although we did not specifically ask any of our sources about this we have seen them referring to more experienced souls taking on altruistic lives that are primarily targeted at the learning of others rather than themselves. In the Introduction I also discussed the idea that more experienced souls are likely to become more involved with training in and practicing altruistic skills. In addition, severe disabilities are held up by Newton and ourselves as a major sign of a progressive learning choice – which is the complete opposite of the traditional Hindu view of them as a punishment for past misdeeds. Nora confirmed this when Andy asked her about these in particular, indicating that they tend to be chosen by more experienced souls who have completed their basic emotional lessons:

> Disabilities usually involve special souls, because it's often very hard, especially when someone can think and feel but not express themselves, so not every soul can handle these sorts of things. They will have learned all the normal lessons, but may have decided to specialize in this sort of work, especially with severe disability.

2.4.2 Why do some people appear to have a blank interlife experience under regression?

In *The Book of the Soul* I sided with those pioneers who report that blank interlife experiences might be assumed to represent souls who either remained totally unaware of their surroundings during their time in the light, or might even have reincarnated from the astral plane without actually entering the light. However, I was unaware of Newton's insistence when training other therapists that these would only be caused by deliberate blocking of the subject from recalling the experience, and our sources were unanimous in supporting this view. Here are Veronica, Alva, Amy, Nora and Denise:

> While there is always an understanding at the soul level, it may be that upon incarnation a soul does not need to remember what occurred in the spirit realm.

> If this will not help their future development, it will not be shown to them... This is not so much related to their level of experience as to what they need to know at that time.

> When a person is accessing their soul state, they only need to recall what they need in their conscious life – the things that will help them to move forward in their life. So some aspects are blocked.

> Less evolved souls are not meant to remember too much because they have other lessons to learn. But as we progress, we remember more and can do more, the link is stronger and it is easier to access.

> There may be more understanding needed, or the soul may have chosen to forget, or for some it is just difficult to find their way between lives...

Sometimes it's too hard to reconnect, it requires a lot of energy, and often a difficult choice in life… More experienced souls tend to remember more between-life details, as well as those who plan to be able to reconnect after they come down, as part of the reawakening.

This latter comment from Denise raises the interesting issue of whether having interlife regression is somehow 'cheating' on our life lessons. But she seems to make it clear that allowing some people to access their interlife memories is a deliberate development designed to assist our 'reawakening', of which more in section 3.4. However this does not alter the fact that for others the experience will be wholly or partly blocked, and this has nothing to do with their ability to attain the requisite depth of trance.

One other point to reconsider is my previous assumption in *The Book of the Soul* that children who spontaneously recall their past lives are more likely to be relatively inexperienced souls because they seem to return swiftly in earth terms and mention few if any details about any sort of interlife experience. However it is clear that, in line with the above evidence about blank interlife regression experiences, this view too requires revision. On the one hand, as we will see in section 4.2, time is experienced differently in the light realms. So an apparently brief between-lives interlude in earth years, as evidenced by some of Ian Stevenson's child subjects, is in fact no guarantee that the experience was in any way curtailed. On the other, a child would be unlikely to be allowed to spontaneously recall details of the interlife because it would be too much for them to take on consciously at such an early age. Indeed this is why details tend only to be uncovered when an adult seeks interlife regression as a deliberate choice and at an age where they are better equipped to handle any information that comes through. As for children who carry over birthmarks and defects, although we saw in section 1.7 that sometimes they may make this choice deliberately, it may nevertheless be reasonable to continue to assume a certain lack of experience in such cases.

2.4.3 Can interlife regression experiences be projections to help us rather than genuine memories?

In line with our enquiry into the extent to which past-life memories can be projections manufactured by spirit guides and others to help us with certain lessons, we asked our sources the same question about interlife recall. Claire repeated that it is important to be aware that this is possible, but Amy, Denise, Katrine and Alva all agreed that most interlife experiences are genuine:

> Generally what is experienced is real.

> On the level that you are working with it will be real, but how it is presented to them will be based on the choices they made in the spirit world.

> Sometimes, but only occasionally, maybe as little as three percent… Usually, the soul will have a lot of memories to take from.

> They are real, at least in so far as a human can experience what is real and what isn't.

Of course what these responses do show, however, is that our recall of interlife experiences can only approximate to the real thing, and must be filtered through our human understanding.

Post-Reincarnation Development

2.5 What happens to souls once they no longer need to reincarnate?

In the last section we saw that there are probably myriad aspects of – and levels in – the light realms, where souls engage in a huge variety of different activities. Some of these will, of course, be souls who are no longer active in the reincarnation cycle, but who remain thoroughly involved in gaining more experience and balance as part of the constant recycling back to the Source. Indeed, one of the mistaken facets of older reincarnatory models seems to be the suggestion that once we have completed the reincarnation cycle we are free to return to the Source, because all the modern evidence suggests that this only marks the beginning of a far longer process. David made the following comparison between the time span of the reincarnation cycle and that of further progress in the light realms:

> That's just the start… It's like the difference between being an adult and a baby – and an adult with a very long life.

We have also seen in section 2.3 that Naomi reported how each soul is created for a specialist purpose, which suggests that we will be constantly preparing ourselves for any eventual role we will undertake in the light realms. Furthermore Newton talks extensively about still-reincarnating subjects engaging in a variety of specialist training between lives as healers, teachers, guides, energy workers and designers or creators – or, as we call them, altruistic skills. Amy reinforced this idea of developing natural propensities as follows:

> You can become anything you want, but it depends on your level of ability, and your natural propensity for certain learning and training. And your guide will monitor that all the way along. It's as if from way back the experiences that you have on the earth plane will add to who you are as a soul in such a way that your natural accumulated gifts and abilities are developed and they create your choices... From way back you move into a pattern of specialism relevant to your natural abilities and gifts. Souls try different things, but your inner core somehow guides you along a certain developmental pathway.

2.5.1 What roles can more experienced souls take?

As to the roles themselves, most of our sources tended merely to indicate that there are many possibilities. Here are Alva, Denise, Claire and Naomi:

> There's quite a few things that can happen. They can incarnate on another planet, they can become teachers, they can join a new group of similar soul energies.

> There are many choices in the spirit realms. Some choose to connect with humans to offer help and guidance, some help those in spirit.

> There are an infinite number of other experiences at different levels of energy vibration.

> There's a wealth of things they can do. In essence all spirits who have finished reincarnating will become teachers in some shape or form. They become spirit guides, or they may help other souls, or they may go to other dimensions.

However David was a little more specific:

> There is much teaching to be done, decisions need to be made about how things will progress, planets need to be changed to provide new lifeforms and environments for souls to incarnate into – all these provisions need to be put in place. And there is much more as well... It's part of the natural progression to train as guides, healers, explorers, storers of knowledge, and so on.

While Veronica tended to concentrate on earth-related activities such as keeping an eye on developments in general, or assisting those still in the reincarnation cycle, she also emphasized that there tends to be a great deal of overlap between roles in the latter category:

There are those who give guidance, those who help to heal, those who facilitate. But again, spirit is multi-faceted, and can be a guide and a teacher and a healer and a facilitator all in one, and draw upon whatever tool is needed for each aspect of its work. There are some that choose to dedicate a part of themselves to helping to raise the energy of the earth, to channeling through specific energy vibrations to help humanity to develop and move forward. There are others who choose to devote more of their energy to help souls as they pass through, either into or out of the spirit realm.

Andy particularly asked Naomi and Nadine about training as a spirit guide, and they agreed that this is a lengthy process:

Guides are specialized souls who have to go through an enormous amount of training.

Quite a lot of souls will take the path of being guides. But it takes quite a long time to understand the subtleties of guiding someone on the physical plane, because you have to learn a lot about mental awareness and connection and the transference of information.

Nadine also reported that it takes even longer to progress to being an elder:

It takes a very, very, very long time. Eventually everybody will be at that level, and many souls are transforming themselves into ones with knowledge, but we have a long way to go.

Amy confirmed that we are all working towards this level, but she also seemed to suggest that, while most guides may still be reincarnating as part of the normal cycle, elders would have succeeded in attaining full spiritual balance in the physical plane:

They would have reached a point in their life experience in physical incarnations where they always acted from their soul awareness. Everything would then be seen and felt from that place, rather than from the personality, because they would have overcome or superseded personality issues. And, no matter what the situation, they would be able to maintain a calm, balanced soul perspective on everything. It's quite difficult to get this level of information, you can only touch on their experience... Different people give them different names. To some they are called the ascended ones, or masters of light, to some they're even known as the angelic realm.

Andy then pressed her for more information on the different types of elder:

Different groups of elders work within different frequencies, with different purposes and potentials... There are those that work specifically with developments on earth, because they have that particular knowledge and training... And there are others with more knowledge and wisdom that support these in turn... But it's not a hierarchy, it's more an expanded awareness.

Nora reinforced this by discussing the idea of elders continuing to learn as well as teach, so that they are supported by ever higher levels:

Some work as teachers or on councils, they work their way up the pyramid. They are learning and teaching at the same time... They still work in a group, and have their own council, it's similar to how it is when you are reincarnating on earth. There's always a council above them to help, they talk amongst themselves to learn as well, they still have classrooms and so on. The groups get smaller and smaller the higher up you go, and it all takes a long time.

Finally Katrine provided a few details about what she referred to as 'teachers':

Teachers operate in the spirit realms with different soul groups, and have specialized areas of expertise. Or they can teach on a one-to-one basis, for example helping an incarnate soul to connect to the spirit realms and their intuitive side more easily than in another life. There are also experienced souls who teach by incarnating even though they might not seem to be such on the earth plane. You can teach just by the way you live – how you think, how you talk, how you treat other people.

This again suggests that the most experienced souls in incarnation probably teach quietly and by example, rather than by proclaiming themselves loudly. Indeed, this again raises the whole issue of experienced souls who *choose* to reincarnate to help humanity and our planet even though they no longer *need* to – who may well be more at the level of elders than guides. This is a common idea supported by all our sources, and it is normally assumed that historical figures such as Moses, Buddha, Jesus, Mohammed and so on would fall into this category. But we should remember that there have probably been thousands more that we have never even heard about – who have worked away quietly, without drawing attention to themselves, and with total disregard for achieving any sort of earthly recognition.

Experiencing Other Planets

2.6 Can souls from earth gain experience on other planets?

At various times I have mentioned the idea that earth is not the only inhabited planet in the universe. Although modern astronomers are still uncertain about the extent of earth's uniqueness as a planet capable of playing home to complex lifeforms, many of the pioneers' subjects indicate that we cannot afford to take a purely geocentric view.

I suggested briefly in section 2.1 that there are a number of options to be considered. Souls might choose to gain the bulk of their reincarnatory experience on another planet, although for this to be most effective it would have to be fully physical like earth. Or a soul that regularly reincarnated on earth or another physical planet might also choose to gain occasional experience of reincarnating on another less physical planet. But they might also gain between-lives experience of another physical planet by merely *visiting* its astral plane. Meanwhile there may also be some planetary dimensions that are so nonphysical that reincarnation as we know it is impossible, in which case these would be experienced in other ways.

Perhaps unsurprisingly, the majority of our sources were unanimous that souls who have chosen to gain most of their reincarnatory experience on earth can indeed gain additional experience in other planetary realms.

2.6.1 What is the nature of life on other planets? Are any of them comparable to the earth experience?

Our attempts to establish the exact nature of these other planets and dimensions that 'human' souls can either incarnate in, or merely gain some sort of non-reincarnatory experience of, proved somewhat more complex. A number of our sources did agree that *some* of these other planetary environments are somewhat different, and apparently less physical, than earth. Here are Veronica, Denise, Amy and Naomi:

> There are other planets where everything is more in energy form, where consciousness is able to present itself in different forms.

> It may not be incarnating into a form as such, but a part of the consciousness travels... It may not be a life as you know it. They can visit for a very short time to experience the space and the different energies.

> As part of your training you can gain experiences and abilities in different systems that you can't get in other places. Depending on what their

specialism is, some souls might choose another system just like choosing a school. Or some might just go for a break, to get away and do something restful, because sometimes variety helps to take away the sameness of incarnating on the earth plane all the time.

Some planetary systems are more akin to the spiritual realm, they are only one step removed from being here. Others are more mental.

When Andy asked Alva to describe the nature of life on one of the other planets, she seemed to pick up on a similar type of environment to that mentioned by Naomi:

I'm getting a picture now. The souls don't materialize in a physical form as we know it. It's like a place for integration, and a place for learning of course… It is more similar to the spirit world. It's a 'One' experience, of functioning as One rather than being an individual.

We have already seen that various pioneers discuss the idea of souls visiting other planets. But as far as I am aware none of them have specifically reported on Naomi's additional suggestion that these nonphysical environments are at least in part targeted towards providing an easy, early-learning experience for new souls *before* they commence the reincarnation cycle on earth:

There are numerous spiritual dimensions, which are places to adapt from being away from the Source, but you are still very much in tune… You are not in a physical body, you are more of a spiritual being. Perhaps if you imagine yourself in a dream, you are not in a physical body but you are aware of your existence. So in these dimensions you know the Source is there, and therefore there is less fear. There is considerable scope for growth for junior souls in these levels, because they have an understanding that they are separate from but still close to the Source… There's a lot of teaching about understanding different conscious and emotional levels, and the importance of, for example, love. There's also play, and just an understanding of beauty.

However Naomi herself also indicated that such early-learning environments could be physical, and therefore allow the experience of death, while Amy corroborated the idea:

The souls in other physical realities are also more connected to the Source. But they are gaining an understanding of what it is to live and die, while having less fear of death.

There are other physical planets that have other challenges… Some are not quite so difficult. They can provide practice for younger souls to acclimatize to the physical before coming here for the first time. Or they can help if somebody is planning to have a particularly difficult lifetime.

Katrine confirmed the idea of 'retreats for younger souls', although without indicating whether such planets would be physical or not. Meanwhile David, although not mentioning early-learning, agreed that 'many other planets are easier' and can be used as something of a rest from the earth environment.

Turning to the second part of this question, it was impossible to gain a definitive view as to whether there are other physical planets that provide an effective alternative to earth as a primary location for the reincarnation experience. Veronica seemed to be emphatic that there are:

> It's the same as incarnating on earth, although there are different energies, issues and understandings to be drawn from different places of incarnation. This is just another choice... Some planets are physical... They have forms that are sometimes very similar to humans, sometimes more like plant forms – that's not to say that they are plants, just that the genetic makeup is more akin to what on earth is vegetation.

Meanwhile Alva seemed to be less certain:

> There are many other planets where you can have a full incarnation. Most souls choose to finish off one experience, for example on earth, first. But there are a few that wish or even *need* to experience something else, then maybe go back to earth.

By contrast Nadine, Katrine, Amy, Claire and Naomi all seemed to maintain that earth provides a relatively unique reincarnation experience:

> They're not really planets, they're forms of thought that have been created. Our solar system is a form of thought, but it's of a lower frequency involving matter.

> The major learning is on planet earth.

> Many other dimensions are not necessarily like ours. They have differences in frequency, vibration, and consciousness. Each experience is different. This one is unique.

> It is possible to incarnate in other physical realities... They are physical but not with human forms... At the current time earth is unique because of the range of experiences and emotions... There is also little memory of being part of the One. There are other physical realities with different vibrations and energy levels which provide an environment where souls can incarnate to experience a different reality and emotions, but earth is unique because of the veil of amnesia that causes the emotions to be so

intense, and this is highly valued at a soul level.

Earth is an old planet that has been through many phases and will go through many more, and it is a very physical planet, so it is very good for teaching at all levels – emotional, physical and spiritual… It's a difficult ground for people to learn on because it can be harsh, and it's difficult for souls to deal with the mental and the physical and the lack of spirituality that you have on earth, but it is also a very rewarding planet with lots of opportunities for real, faster growth Yet other dimensions are useful too… There are other physical realities that are kinder, without the brutality that you can have on earth… But the human lifeform is unique to earth.

Although Nora seemed to be somewhat constrained by lack of personal experience, she too seemed to support earth's uniqueness when she responded as follows: 'I know there are some other places, but I don't know if they are planets or more just energy places… As far as I know, earth comes first.'

I can only conclude from this that, while there may well be other physical planets that provide something of an alternative to earth as a reincarnatory environment, earth may still be somewhat unique in terms of the human lifeform and the depth and range of emotions that can be experienced through it. Nevertheless, this should not imbue us with any false sense of superiority. When Andy asked if there are any planets that are home to more advanced lifeforms than humans, Denise replied 'there are many', while Katrine added the following salutary reminder:

Yes. They might look like humans, but they are more spiritually advanced. Humans measure advancement in terms of technology, but that is not advanced to us.

3

HUMANITY'S PAST AND FUTURE

Our third group of questions shifts the focus very much towards humanity and events on earth in general. We will look at the origins of humanity, the idea of lost civilizations like Atlantis, the logistics of how soul numbers keep pace with massive population increases, and at what the future might hold for humanity. The first two sections in particular considerably broaden the scope, moving away from the strictly spiritual matters we have so far dealt with, and into prehistoric territory about which myriads of books have been written and theories concocted.

The Emergence of the Human Race

3.1 When did the modern human race first emerge?

Our starting point must be the origins of the modern human race, which immediately places us in controversial territory. As I discussed at some length in *Genesis Unveiled*, using a neo-Darwinian evolutionary model modern archaeologists have been steadily pushing back the date for the emergence of *Homo sapiens*, so that it is now generally reckoned to be somewhere in the region of 150–200,000 years ago. However this is almost certainly not the same as the point at which modern humans made what I regard as their defining intellectual, cultural and spiritual breakthrough – when they started to think about their own mortality and what, if anything, might happen to them after death. For this I focused on the earliest evidence of deliberate human burial, which so far comes from Israel and dates to about 100,000 years ago.

By contrast, for decades there have been alternative authors who insist

– usually on the basis of what have come to be known as 'anomalous' or 'out-of-place' artifacts, and other skeletal and ancillary evidence – that modern humans have been around for millions of years. As fascinating as much of this material is at first glance, in *Genesis Unveiled* I came to the conclusion that the underlying scholarship is rarely of sufficient quality to mount a genuine challenge to the orthodoxy.

Andy and I knew in advance that we would be on tricky ground, because soul memories tend to work in much the same way as our human memory. It seems that some souls may be good with names or dates from past lives and so on, in just the same way as we are in human life, and others will be less so – perhaps only able to point to the early or late part of a particular century for a given life, for example. So in the current context it was clearly going to be much more difficult for our subjects to be specific about events that stretch back tens or even hundreds of thousands of years, and in which they may have played no personal part as a soul. Furthermore, it would be by no means impossible that our sources themselves might suffer from the same blocks.

Unfortunately our fears proved almost entirely justified, and most answers were highly non-specific. Nora reported that 'human development was really slow, it just developed gradually over time and there was no real point when it changed from one to another'. David suggested 'the biology of it goes back hundreds of thousands of years'. Nadine merely offered 'thousands and thousands of years'. Veronica and Amy both reported that it dates back to 'the ice age' – but this is none too helpful, because the Pleistocene epoch proper began about 1.7 million years ago, while the most recent mini-glaciation commenced between 115,000 and 75,000 years ago, and began retreating about 18,000 years ago to take us into the Holocene epoch. Meanwhile Denise was somewhat enigmatic when she replied 'slightly earlier than you are currently aware – there were small hands before your paintings on the wall'. This seems to be a reference to the type of outlined hand prints that have been found in a number of European cave sites more commonly associated with shamanic paintings and geometric shapes, although their dates remain relatively recent and still fall within the boundaries of the 'Upper Paleolithic explosion' of around 40,000 years ago.

What we can take from this is that none of them seem to be suggesting that the modern human race was in existence *millions* of years ago, which appears to put paid to the more outlandish suggestions of alternative researchers. Moreover, the only one who did place a date on our emergence – albeit that she seemed entirely surprised by what she was saying, and subsequently confirmed her total lack of prior knowledge of this topic – was Alva: 'In human earth years I'm getting 90,000. Is that possible?' Although our question was aimed at the general date of emergence, and not specifically the date at which humans first started to become spiritual beings, it is not impossible that the proximity of this date to my estimate for the latter of 100,000 years ago may be more than just coincidence.

3.1.1 Were there experiments to bring advanced soul energy into the earth plane before the human form evolved?

In fact in many respects I was far more interested in the spiritual development of our planet in general, rather than in specifically focusing on the human race. I surmised in *Genesis Unveiled* that, because of the apparent differentiation between animal and human soul energy, with the latter being far more individualized, there may have been experiments to bring what I refer to as 'advanced' or 'human-style' soul energy into incarnation before the human race had fully evolved on planet earth.

There were two main drivers behind this theory. On the one hand, many of the Near Eastern traditional texts discuss the idea of 'fallen angels' – although I would argue that the versions we have now have confused a number of different historical and spiritual themes. Nevertheless, one of these appears to be the idea that some of these 'angels' were overly anxious to 'descend' to earth, seemingly against the advice of their fellows and before time. On the other hand, a number of the 'creation of man' traditions from around the world seem to hint at the idea that a series of unsuccessful experiments took place before an appropriate 'model' was finally produced. Could these reports have been describing a process of trial and error, whereby advanced soul energies experimented by incarnating in a variety of pre-human species before the modern human race evolved? Moreover, could it be that these were unsuccessful precisely because these species were insufficiently advanced from a physiological, neurological and psychological perspective to provide a proper vehicle for their relatively high level of spiritual energy and awareness?

As I mentioned in *Genesis Unveiled*, it was only after I had written the entire first draft of its manuscript that I discovered Michael Newton's work, and was amazed to find his report that some subjects confirmed this idea of pre-human soul experiments. However we should note that his report is brief, consisting of two short sentences only. Moreover this theory has rarely been discussed by other researchers, apart from Hans TenDam making a brief reference to a small number of regression subjects experiencing life millions of years ago as large primates, and in one case even a dinosaur – and, of the relevant subjects, only Denise had read his work. Nor, remember, had any of them read *Genesis Unveiled*. So I was again surprised and delighted when a number of our sources not only corroborated this idea but added a significant degree of detail. Here are Claire, Nora, Nadine, Katrine and Denise:

> The experiment of incarnating on earth has been repeated several times.

> There were what we call experiments now, but they didn't work out too well, and it took some time to establish what sort of lifeform would have the best chance of learning... It was a process of trial and error... From the tiniest first lifeform there were souls, but they were really, really simple... Then there were these really big lifeforms a long time ago, in the water, in the air and on land. They evolved quickly physically, but they just didn't learn... Their ability to express emotions, to look to the future and remember the past, and to exercise free will, were all insufficiently developed.

> Experiments – that's the wrong word – projects were devised to see if a soul, and the awareness of the soul, could live on the earth plane. But even though some were able to keep the energetic form around them, the density of the energy on the earth plane created a distortion, and because of this the soul was not able to function in the form that was originally intended.

> They experimented on both human and animals, but they found out that humans would be the right way to go. They would evolve more quickly, and souls were able to join the human form much more easily and with much less resistance.

> There were experiments, but they didn't go well. There was heaviness and unhappiness... The soul felt lost and abandoned, with no capacity for faith, because areas of the brain were missing.

But all this begs the question of how the human form was arrived at. Was it purely via an evolutionary process? From a general perspective, Newton refers to 'designer souls' who develop the blueprints for the different animal, vegetable and mineral lifeforms throughout the universe by using thought-forms and directed energy in one way or another. Admittedly the suggestion seems to be that these are constantly evolving in different planetary environments along natural evolutionary lines, but he also provides one example of a subject working to correct a serious imbalance between the dominant animal and plant lifeforms in the ecosystem of another planet – giving evolution a 'nudge' in the right direction so that the experiment did not have to start afresh. All this seems to represent a fine spiritual explanation of the 'intelligent design' process.

So was this process used in developing the human form? Nora was unsure, merely reporting: 'I don't know how they did this, but they found another lifeform that had far greater brain capacity and capacity for emotions, that had much better potential – and here we are.' Nadine hinted at something more when she suggested that 'the physical form had to be reformed again'. But Alva indicated that the evolution of the human form was always planned:

> The earth was originally sent new energies, like little seeds or vibrations to begin with for simple lifeforms. And this was from the Oneness, so it also contained the experience of other lifeforms... The environment was set so that various forms could exist, as another sort of experiencing... But there was always a plan for a human-type form to be in place on earth, although first the right plant and animal forms had to be in place to support their basic needs. So human evolution did happen over a long earthly time, because it had to be born out of the animal forms that developed.

Denise reinforced the idea that intelligent design was involved by specifically mentioning the idea of a blueprint:

> There was adaptation... Additions were made to the brain... Deliberate change was set in place by the incarnating soul energies that held the blueprint, which then allowed evolution to work... On many levels, the energies worked together to allow the system to work as a whole.

But Naomi provided the fullest details, not only of the experiments that were conducted in the physical plane, but also of how designs were tried out in the light realms first:

> We did try other animals, that was fully investigated... Souls visited the planet, and we looked at the options. There were a number of experiments undertaken in the spirit world. Because everything is created in the spirit world as well, you have creators who can create trees or bushes or human beings or whatever. It's difficult to tell how well a soul is going to adapt until it is actually put into a body, but you can do various tests, which we did. But I don't know much more about that, except that humans ended up being the best animals to house a human-type soul.

Nevertheless, none of this necessarily implies that there is a human-type blueprint in use on other planets as well – as I suggested in *The Book of the Soul*, based primarily on evidence from TenDam. In section 2.6 we had difficulty gaining a definitive view on this issue, and further questioning here did not appear to help. Katrine provided the following information, although it was not clarified further:

> Before earth there were other planets but their civilizations died out. So we had to find another planet. Souls always find a new planet when an old one dies out. But earth is one of the best places for the soul to evolve quickly, in the human form.

Meanwhile Alva indicated that, although the prearranged plan for a human form on earth was in part fulfilled by evolution, in addition 'other human lifeforms were brought in from the Source and from other places in the universe'. However again her exact meaning is not entirely clear. This, coupled with the general shortage of relevant comments from our sources, means that for now we should probably retain an open mind as to whether the human form is merely an earthly blueprint or has wider applicability.

Lost Civilizations

Note that Veronica was not asked any of these questions.

3.2 Are any of the myths of lost continents and civilizations true?

Even orthodox archaeologists have been increasingly forced to push back the period in which large, farming-based, permanent, stone-built settlements first emerged. The earliest, which are found in eastern Turkey and Syria, now date back as far as 11,500 years ago. But what about the persistent speculation that there may have been earlier civilizations that were destroyed?

David's brief but enigmatic response was that 'there have been civilizations that have been destroyed, but humans know of them'. But Denise threw her weight entirely behind the proposition, raised by both Newton and myself independently, that they were not on earth and therefore only soul memories:

> They are soul memories… They existed in another dimension on a different level, a sister to the earth. It had a wonderful vibration, but there was no place for it near earth with human heaviness… So the sphere moved away to ensure that frequencies that were so pure and high could remain that way. But it shimmers still.

Alva too supported this idea, although she had some prompting from Andy, including the mention of the name 'Atlantis'. And although a number of our sources used the same terminology without prompting, they also indicated that this name does not really mean anything in the light realms having only been coined by modern humans:

> It's not earth as such, as we think it is. It's not like a lump of land that's disappeared.
> *Could Atlantis, for example, be on a different planet?*
> Just to me, now, it seems like that makes sense... It's like a memory that we brought with us.

Meanwhile Nora seemed to adopt a more halfway approach whereby Atlantis initially developed on earth, but was soon transferred to another realm:

> The one they call Atlantis evolved quickly in terms of energy work, but not in emotions and so on... When it didn't work another energy creation realm was found for this work to continue, and they took all the souls back in a natural way after the human forms died... The humans that followed on earth no longer had this knowledge and had to carry on working on emotions and so on.

The remainder of our sources did place a lost civilization exclusively on earth. Furthermore, despite the proliferation of books on this topic – many of which derive from channeled material – it is highly significant that three of our subjects who provided important accounts subsequently confirmed, against our expectations, that they had not read anything about it. They are Naomi, Nadine and Katrine:

> Atlantis did exist, yes. The souls were more spiritually evolved, and they used the energy fields around them to much greater capacity than the current civilization. But they broke the code. They misused their energy powers, their strength and their wisdom, and started affecting how the planet functioned... So they caused their own destruction... It wasn't an island in the way that many people think. That was part of it, but the actual area was much larger.

> Earlier civilizations had more spiritual knowledge, so lots of energy-based technologies were devised. But due to the distortion of the energy field at the time, the technologies were too advanced for that human form, and it unraveled itself... The body was able to understand the technology, but it wasn't developed enough energetically, or sufficiently in tune with the essence of Oneness.

> The Atlanteans evolved very quickly, and they had a lot of powers, but

they had to be destroyed because things were getting out of hand, there was too much misuse of power... The ability to use mind control and read each other's thoughts was very common then. It was like an experiment, we wanted to see if the souls and the humans would all evolve quicker, and all help each other and drag each other up in the right direction. But it got out of control because of free will. And they were not ready for that. People got greedy and very cruel, and very into that power. And they couldn't handle it.

Amy provided somewhat more detail on the same lines – and while she subsequently confirmed she had read widely on the subject, she also indicated that she had 'always struggled with it':

Atlantis was a consciousness, a way of existing within the energy of the planet. It was made up of many different places, peoples and cultures, so it had a far-ranging influence. But it's not the *where* of Atlantis that's important, it's the *how* and the *why*... It was no different to any other cultural evolution on the planet in that it peaked and then died. But it seeded a particular kind of consciousness in humanity. Its purpose was to bring an awareness that if you tamper with, misuse or disrespect earth energies then that has consequences for the planet. Because in many ways our own culture is taking the same path, so the race memory we have of those events is crucial... In Atlantis the number of people who were aware of the deeper mysteries became outgrown by the number who did not. And what we have to learn and remember this time round is to maintain and keep building that knowledge not to misuse the planet, not to continue to destroy certain aspects of it, to work to maintain its stability.

Claire too was forthcoming about what she referred to as Atlantis 1 and 2. But in her subsequent feedback she indicated that she had read more about known ancient civilizations in general than the lost civilization of Atlantis in particular, and had certainly not read anything about Atlantean spirituality:

In the initial experiments incarnating souls had some awareness of who they were, but they failed and were brought to an end. They were repeated with three different civilizations on earth before the current one... The last one was Atlantis, although the one before that was similar so you could call them Atlantis 1 and 2... The idea you currently have of Atlantis is not completely correct. Civilization was widespread, not just in one place or island. It was more spiritually advanced than now... Thought communication was possible for some, although not everyone was at the same level. They were still aware of who they were as part of the One, and realized they were co-creators to a certain extent... But there were some who became greedy and were not acting for the benefit of their fellow man, so the experiment was brought to an end. There were some memories of what had been achieved as the new civilization developed, but the veil grew thicker and with time people forgot who they were, and what they were capable of... That's why so many different cultures had the same ideas about the Source.

These reports clearly share a number of common themes, all of which corroborate important ideas I put forward in *Genesis Unveiled*. First, although none of our sources attempted to place a date on either the emergence or destruction of Atlantis, this is not only consistent with the dating problems discussed in the previous section, but it also means that by default none of them suggested dates that are massively out of step with conventional ideas of human evolution. Second, they all emphasized that its inhabitants were at least initially highly advanced in terms of their spirituality and energy manipulation abilities, and made no mention of any sort of advanced technology commensurate with our own – despite that fact that even most esoteric and channeled sources tend to link these two together. Third, they all agreed with the commonly expressed view that the Atlantean experiment went awry, leading ultimately to its destruction. However, Amy in particular corroborated my suggestion that the real lesson for us to heed from their experience is not the location of this former civilization, but its descent from a state of high spirituality into a maelstrom of materialism, greed and disrespect for the planet and its other inhabitants. Meanwhile Claire specifically asserted that a variety of the ancient cultures in our most recent epoch had 'the same ideas about the Source'. This seems to support my attempt in *Genesis Unveiled* to demonstrate the profound spiritual insights that lie at the heart of all the 'origin traditions' from around the globe, which seem hitherto to have been overlooked by conventional scholars.

Amy was also one of only two sources who made specific reference to a civilization older than that of Atlantis, using the name 'Lemuria', although she subsequently confirmed she had read a fair bit about both. Her description seemed to be pointing to a totally different order of being and soul energy:

> The Lemurians, who were an older evolution than Atlantis, worked with thought streams. They had one collective unconscious, and each different civilization had to learn a different facet of that overall consciousness. But they knew that they were connected to that greater consciousness, and to each other. So they didn't work or think on the level that humans do now, they were on a different level completely. They worked more in the

realms of creating with the power of consciousness. They were able to do and think about things in a completely different way, but just as they had incredible power to be positive with their thoughts, they also had incredible power to do the opposite with them, through fear... They were incarnate, just with a different level of physicality... They were taller, much slimmer, and less muscular. They didn't have very physical lives, they lived very much in their head. So everything evolved from their thinking. They were on a much higher level, but only in terms of what they could achieve with the power of the mind, and consciousness in general. So it was vastly different from our way of living. But the lid is shut on that part for us, it's not something we could even begin to understand. Most of those souls are far more ancient than any soul on earth at the moment.

Despite a distinct lack of prior knowledge, Claire also referred to the spirituality of the Lemurians briefly, although again emphasizing that this name has merely been adopted by modern humans and does not signify anything because 'they had no need of a name for their reality in their terms of reference'. In particular she mentioned the way in which they ended their civilization: 'They were so aware of who they really were that it was a common agreement to end the reality of that civilization without physical intervention.' By contrast, she reports that the two 'Atlantean experiments' did require physical intervention:

> The last Atlantis ended in a physical disaster, a fireball or meteorite. The one before that was again a physical disaster – an opening up of the earth's crust... Each of these was a group decision made when things were not going according to plan... It was made by those souls taking part in the experiment that remained in the spirit realms, who were themselves the creators of it... Just by thinking they caused it, by group consensus thought.

In *Genesis Unveiled* I laid out the textual and geological evidence for there having been a worldwide catastrophe some time around 11,500 years ago, which wiped out all traces of our antediluvian forebears. I also argued that this was caused by a large meteorite crashing into the sea off the south-east coast of North America, although using the term 'universal karma' to describe the underlying process of ending the experiment to allow a fresh start. But in fact we can now see that 'collective karma' might be a better description, because Claire is adamant that in both the Atlantean and Lemurian experiments it was the souls *themselves* who were involved who took the decision to end them. And for me this apparent democracy has a certain resonance.

Claire was also the only source who consistently referred to the veil of amnesia, which as we saw in the Introduction is the mechanism by which our level of connectedness to and memory of the light realms while incarnate is regulated. When the veil is lowered we remember less, and vice versa. An idea briefly mooted by some of Newton's subjects is that the veil has been lowered in the last few thousand years as part of a deliberate policy of experimentation originating in the light realms. And while a number of our sources merely confirmed the general idea of the Atlanteans being, at least originally, more spiritually aware, several others seemed to support this idea of a deliberate reduction in soul awareness. For example, Katrine reported above that in the Atlantean 'experiment' they 'had a lot of powers' but 'were not ready for that'; Nora that they were more 'evolved in terms of energy work', while those that came after 'no longer had this knowledge'; and Claire that they were 'aware they were part of the One', but for their successors the 'veil grew thicker'. So perhaps the rules of the human experiment were indeed changed after the last catastrophe.

Of course, all the material in this section could represent a heady concoction of conscious interference and imagination. However the lack of prior knowledge of ancient civilizations reported by a number of our subjects suggests that we would be wrong to dismiss them out of hand. So, on the basis that they *may* have some validity, I should attempt to put them into some sort of coherent framework.

It appears that the first or 'Lemurian evolution' of souls were a totally different order of being, who were less physical and perhaps rather more a pure energy projection. This not only allowed them full rein to use the power of their thoughts and soul energy, but it also means they could have been on the planet long before the modern human race developed. In addition they had a more collective consciousness, which was more fully connected to and aware of the Source, but their lack of full involvement in the physical world restricted their ability to gain experience.

Then the modern human form finally emerged, probably with a degree of behind-the-scenes prompting from the light realms. This 'Atlantean evolution' began with a wave of genuine incarnations in which souls retained their soul awareness to a significant degree, albeit that the merger with a fully physical human form and brain would have introduced significant restrictions compared to the Lemurian experience. This would account for the widespread ancient traditions of a 'Golden Age' of spirituality, which I discussed at length in *Genesis Unveiled* –

100

and if my evolutionary and archaeological estimates are correct it would have occurred no earlier than 100,000 years ago, or thereabouts.

However this evolution too was not without its problems. Some people started to use their telepathic, mind control and other energy manipulation abilities for entirely selfish ends. This tendency became increasingly prevalent until the situation was completely out of hand, and a general soul consensus was reached that the experiment should be brought to an end by a major physical catastrophe, some time around 11,500 years ago. At this point a deliberate plan was put in place to reduce our soul awareness somewhat, precisely so that these more spiritual and energetic powers could no longer be abused and cause widespread disruption. However, as we will see in section 3.4, our own 'modern evolution' has not exactly proved an unqualified success, and it may be that the experiment is about to change again.

The Soul Logistics of Population Increase

3.3 How is the exponential human population increase on earth being satisfied from a soul perspective?

One of the issues that seems to bother more rational people when they are first presented with the idea of reincarnation is how does the number of souls keep pace with the exponentially increasing human population on earth. Nora was unusual in that she did express some concern as follows: 'That's one of the things we are working on. Population expansion is too fast, it has to slow down.' However the remainder of our sources were all agreed that only from an entirely human and geocentric perspective could one ever think that this could be a problem. Here are David, Veronica, Katrine, Denise, Claire and Amy:

> There is no restriction on the infinite... The soul energy used by the earth is a tiny fraction of the whole. There is so much more.

> There is infinite energy, there are infinite resources, there are infinite sparks that are known as souls.

> There are a lot more souls than humans, so this is not a problem.

> There are infinite souls. The stock is constantly replenished and renewed at Source.

> There is always enough soul energy for reincarnation.

> The number of souls is limitless. It's limited human thinking to worry that

there aren't enough souls for human bodies.

So what are the underlying factors that ensure that population explosion does not cause logistics problems? The idea that animal souls regularly progress into human souls has already been discounted in section 2.2, but in *The Book of the Soul* I indicated that there are three main mechanisms at work – and, as far as I am aware, no other researcher has analyzed this issue in similar detail. But before we discuss each of these mechanisms in turn, we should note Alva's general reminder that any increase in the number of souls available via them is at least to some extent offset by more experienced souls graduating from the 'earthly round'.

3.3.1 Are new human souls still being created?

The first mechanism is, of course, via new human souls being created on a regular basis. We saw in section 2.3 that the majority of our sources support this view, and they added little more information here except that, when asked by Andy if she could give a proportion of souls on this planet that are in their first incarnations, Alva suggested 'about five percent'. Meanwhile Nora continued with her rather more concerned stance, suggesting that 'it takes longer for new souls to grow than it does to create a new human child'.

3.3.2 Are souls coming back with greater frequency?

The second mechanism is that, by taking shorter interlife breaks in earth years, souls can reincarnate more frequently to satisfy population increases. The pioneers do provide some evidence to support this proposition, albeit that there are huge problems with interpreting their limited data. But when we put it to our sources, Denise rejected it, while Alva and Nora accepted it, all without further comment.

Meanwhile Amy agreed with it 'because the changes are so big', Claire did the same but only because there is a 'willingness for the present experiment to progress', while Katrine rejected it but then said it would happen 'if' souls wanted to evolve more quickly'. This concentration on other reasons for an increased frequency of reincarnation seemed to be in line with their general lack of concern about population logistics.

3.3.3 Are more souls from other planets or dimensions incarnating on earth?

The third mechanism is that more souls who normally frequent other planets or dimensions can come to earth, as we might expect given the ability of earthly souls to go in the other direction. Our sources were unanimous that this can happen, and only Claire put any sort of rider on it:

> In order to reincarnate on earth the frequency of vibration has to adjust. To some extent souls at different vibration levels have their own realities to experience, so there is no need for crossing over, and souls with a completely different frequency would not be able to join the earth experiment. But there are some whose frequency is only slightly higher who are able, and have chosen, to incarnate on earth.

But when we turn to the issue of why they might do this – although Veronica was generally insistent that 'the focus is on the development of earth rather than other places at the moment, so more resources are available to it' – again our sources' main focus was not so much on population logistics but on other reasons. Nadine and Veronica cited the now familiar answer 'to gain experience'. David and Alva did likewise, but the former added 'to raise their level of challenge if they have been on easier planets', while the latter reported 'what's special on earth is the emotions, the love energy, the empathy and a particular sense of joy'. Naomi too said it could be to gain experience 'to hasten their spiritual advancement', but also that 'some souls have come from a planet that can no longer sustain life'. Meanwhile a number of our sources also suggested that more experienced souls from other places are currently incarnating on earth in an attempt to assist us with major challenges and changes that we currently face, and we will consider their comments in the next section.

When Andy asked what proportion of souls currently incarnating on earth come from other planets, their responses were mixed, as they so often were when faced with a quantitative question. Amy replied 'about fifteen percent, which is higher than usual, but still not as high as it could be or has been in previous episodes' – although she seemed to partly contradict this elsewhere by saying 'I don't feel that there's any major influx because this is humanity's lesson'. Naomi seemed to be going along similar lines when she reported that there are 'many'. But Alva replied 'very small, maybe as little as one or two percent', supported by Nadine with 'not very many'.

Andy also asked whether being on earth could cause problems for a soul coming from elsewhere because, for example, Newton makes great play of what he calls 'hybrid souls' having problems adapting to the earth environment – with one of his subjects even indicating that they often end up as prime candidates for remodeling. Veronica alone suggested their experience would be no different. But Amy reported that 'the density of the earth and of the physical body could be a challenge', while Nadine reported that 'sometimes they might have problems with their connection with other people, and with other energy forms, because their level of energy and frequency is slightly different'. David and Alva went into more detail about the possible problems they might face:

> Earth is a very heavy planet, especially in terms of emotions. Humanity is at a time of great crisis in terms of growth – it is a young adolescent, and young adolescents can be creative but also destructive. So coming here from a relatively easy world, they might find all this hard to deal with… And there can be all sorts of physical symptoms, like skin complaints, or problems with vision or breathing. Just as we were talking earlier about physical injuries being carried across, so can physical traits from these other physical worlds. It all depends on how much of their energy from their previous lives has been brought along.

> They don't always understand the human reaction pattern, or the combination of feelings and thoughts and behaviors… The physical body may not function very well… They can have psychological problems with dissociation from this life, from their feelings, from thoughts… But they've chosen this particular incarnation for a particular reason.

All this sounds rather dismal for these poor souls from elsewhere. However when Andy pressed Alva as to whether they would be more likely to behave abnormally, for example committing repeated murders, she seemed fairly noncommittal – and she certainly suggested that if they did they would be given plenty of chances to put things right, just like any other soul.

In passing I must make an apology to those who are fascinated by the idea of contact between physical extraterrestrials and earth, either in the distant past or in the current era. This is an area of heated debate, but I have always supported the increasingly popular view that there is a significant overlap between supposedly physical close encounters and abductions, and more spiritual phenomena involving altered states of consciousness. It is because this is such an involved topic, and I really felt we could not do it justice alongside all our other areas of interest, that I excluded it from our research.

Having studied the three possible mechanisms by which souls might satisfy the rapid increase in human population, we must nevertheless admit failure in our attempt to gain any statistics about which mechanisms are most in use at present. It may be that the retrieval of such information is just not suited to our research process, but this is clearly an area that could receive further attention in future. It is interesting not so much because of logistics issues, but because it would be fascinating to learn more about the proportions of new, experienced and originally non-human souls across the globe.

Humanity's Present Problems and Possible Futures

3.4 What is the biggest problem facing humanity at the moment?

On the face of it this question requires no specialist knowledge, and anyone could quite happily provide an answer that suited them. Moreover, we will find that our sources were generally unanimous that great changes are upon us, and that we can either rise to the challenge or continue on our path of destruction – a view taken by reactionaries in every generation in every epoch. But their responses did not reflect a standard expression of doom and gloom. They all offered some highly insightful deconstructions of our current situation, as well as important advice about the future – some of which we will not consider until the final chapter. Above all they balanced any apparent bleakness of outlook with the message that there is everything to play for.

This will be a lengthy section that covers a great deal of ground, but we will start with their opening gambits. Although they tended to focus on different aspects of the issue, all of our sources were united that a lack of spiritual awareness and understanding, and excessive focus on the material world, is the primary problem. Here are David, Veronica, Denise, Amy, Naomi and Nora:

> Self-delusion. And by that we mean humanity seeing itself not as it is but as they are told it is by other humans… If humans can increase their level of understanding about their true nature, then all the other problems will be resolved... Most of the problems are caused by greed, intolerance and prejudice, which is just another expression of fear. When you can see beyond those emotions you will truly learn to grow.

> Themselves… Although there is an increase in the number of incarnating souls who are seeking to understand, to reach a level of awareness and enlightenment, there are still many who aren't. There needs to be work

not only on a soul level but on a conscious level, and that is happening but not completely.

Lack of belief and faith. In large groups the human brain capacity can easily become restricted by worry and greed and physical human existence. Left unaided it becomes a force that ultimately self-destructs, so help is required to reconnect, to remember the soul, to lead the way.

Materialism. In making physical things their master, their god, people are losing their connection with the impulses from their soul for growth and development. They want an easy life, and it can be easy at times, but soul growth is about challenge, and avoiding all of that collectively does no good. They're losing their faith, but if it can be turned around they might find a new faith, new impulses, new belief systems that can be accessed.

If one looks at individuals, there is a lack of love and a lack of intuitive understanding. At the moment there is a real clash between the mind and the spirit. And there is a serious possibility that spirituality will not be sufficiently sought after by the human race, although only through that they will find love and peace.

Life on earth is changing too fast... More and more souls are choosing to go off the path... Humans have stopped thinking about their lovely planet, and instead money and power is more important to them.

Alva's response was along similar lines, but she emphasized the need to *balance* the spiritual and the material:

Lack of stillness... The focus of humans is outwards, on the material things they have created. And the brain has now been programmed to think that its needs are outside of itself. They need a new car, they need a new place to live, they need a certain amount of money, and so on and so forth. But slowly but surely now they understand that they need to balance that outside world with their inside world, with the soul world. They need to learn the value of the inner life... Having said that, some people who are very spiritually minded seem to forget that they also need to balance that with the material world. So everyone must learn to balance the material with the spiritual, that's why they're incarnated on earth. It's too much of a strain, ignoring how the body reacts, not getting a balance between work and relaxation. They need to do things that are good for the soul and the body. They need to find their strength, their value. We were sent here because earth is a beautiful place to be. And if you can't see the beauty and strength in yourself, then you can't see the beauty and strength in nature.

Meanwhile Katrine was more focused on the lack of community:

Lack of compassion... There is selfishness everywhere, and greed. We just need to care about each other, and if we did that all the other things would follow by themselves. But people don't know who their neighbor is, they don't help anybody in the street, they live more and more in their own lives and don't want to bother with anybody else.

Because she had previously mentioned the community spirit of native tribes, Andy then asked her why humanity in general had been allowed to move away from this model of smaller groups living together with common aims and values. She provided an insightful and unexpected answer, especially for those who might long to return to a simpler form of existence:

In the tribes they were more of a group, they were very afraid to be an individual. So it's all about challenge, about letting people come to the edge, forcing them to find the answers within themselves, and not in the people around them. That's why they need to feel isolated and alone.

3.4.1 How is global warming viewed, and what needs to be done?

Our sources tended to demonstrate their full duality when answering this question and the next. Sometimes they allowed their subjective, human perspective to come to the fore, showing genuine concern about global warming and the fate of our beautiful planet. At others their more objective, soul perspective produced a certain detachment, and the view that ultimately it does not really matter what happens to earth and humanity – because the collective soul experiment will continue whether they are around or not. Nevertheless the majority did seem to agree that a large proportion of global warming is man-made, and represents more than just a cyclic fluctuation in earth's climate. They also seemed to infer that this is all part of the test for humanity, and that if we continue to fail it the scale of resulting devastation will increase.

Naomi, David and Nadine most epitomized the more detached stance, although still offering solutions to the problem:

If mankind does not look after the earth and take care of her, she will wreak devastation. And then a new civilization will begin again... There has to be an understanding that the world is finite, and its resources are finite, and if people don't work together as a community then the race could destroy itself.

I think with less concern than on earth. The earth has gone through many changes and will go through many more, and some of the changes will not be easy... There will be death and destruction... But the goal is to help humans to take responsibility for their planet, and that hasn't happened yet... The more the true nature of humankind is evidenced the more it becomes real, and the more it can grow up and past its adolescence. But if it does not reach this level of awareness soon it could well self-destruct.

The world's resources are not being sustained... If humans continue as they are, there will be a kind of 'wash-out'... The earth will do what it needs to do to clean itself up... Human consciousness needs to change to allow it to use the resources in the way they should be used, and then there will be plenty for everyone.

By contrast, Veronica, Denise, Katrine, Alva and Amy were less emphatic about major devastation, and concentrated more on the potential solutions:

If the level of awareness is increased, the actions that have brought about global warming will be discontinued. It will allow such a love of everything that there will be immense earth healing. Humanity will be more careful, more loving towards the earth.

It's a potential issue... Changes will only come about from the bottom to the top, not the top to the bottom. Giving information to those on the ground level will allow them to influence those on the higher level, and it needs small groups and constant conversation to affect big change.

It is happening because of human activity... But also people are feeling too safe, and these natural disasters are there to shake them up, to force them to look at life differently... If people can feel compassion toward each other, they will also feel compassion toward nature and animals and everything around them. They will feel that they need to take care of where they live, not just themselves.

The only thing that will really change it is people's consciousness. What are their real needs? What are they focusing on? What happens when they don't buy stuff anymore? Because the whole of society is built up in this system of buying and selling, changing it can be a terrifying thought. So this needs to go slowly, and it will take many generations yet... At first nature will respond to this unbalanced energy with floods, hurricanes and extreme weather. But this will force humanity to think again, to find their values, maybe to focus on different things in their lives. And then the general consciousness will slowly change, by people actually demanding other values.

It may have gone too far already. Some things are set in motion and can't be stopped, but they can be softened so that less lives are affected, by people working with the earth... People need to come back to the awareness of themselves as part of nature, not above it. Because they're not emotionally connected to nature and to the land on which they live, they have a disregard for it, it has just become a commodity or a possession. They need to come back to a feeling of being part of it, and then they'll respect it more and take care of it and each other.

Amy continued by discussing the need to rebalance the planet's energy fields. Although this is an area in which she works in her conscious life, I feel that her comments about the motivation for and approach to working with ancient energy sites are important:

There are more people working with the planet's energy balance now than ever before, which is giving us a chance to get past the challenge, which we didn't manage last time... The ancient's knowledge is all around, in all of the special sacred places connected to earlier civilizations. And when you are there you can ask for that memory or knowledge and it will be pulled into your energy field... But we have to be careful not to have the wrong motivation... Some people will get involved because they want self-aggrandizement, and to become famous, to be 'the one' that finds the missing link or proves the existence of what went before. But all of those motivations are pretty useless. The purpose of reconnecting with the knowledge is to bring back the awareness of how to work with it so as to be of service to the planet. So the physical structures at these places are not that important, and there's too much focus on that part of it.

If Amy's contentions about these global ancient sites are not merely consciously derived, we must remember that the archaeological evidence to date places them in the modern, post-catastrophe epoch – which, if the propositions from the previous section are correct, has been one of reduced spiritual awareness throughout. This presents the problem as to how our ancient forebears remained sufficiently aware to recognize and work at these energy sites. But we can only assume that, just as at any time, some people would have been more spiritually aware than others. Indeed the concentration of those with a purer spiritual awareness may have been in those communities that remained relatively materially unsophisticated, as opposed to in those that developed into the highly politicized grand civilizations of yesteryear.

3.4.2 Do we need a major global catastrophe to initiate a fresh start?

The correlation between the answers in this and the previous section suggests that, if we are to once again face some sort of major catastrophe to initiate a fresh start, it will arise this time not from a meteorite impact but from our own actions in causing global warming. But our sources' responses again varied. Denise merely reported that 'there is a watershed right now', but Alva and Nadine epitomized a more detached stance by providing very real warnings about the possibility of worldwide catastrophe. Nevertheless they were equally clear that its likelihood and extent lies entirely in human hands:

> There are shifts that have been working for quite a long time already. The Source is sending out big enough waves to make the human race awaken. If that doesn't help, it will be more and more severe... But, as always, it's down to the free will and choices of humanity.

> The earth plane has a consciousness of its own, and outsiders will not interfere with that. So if, in its awareness and consciousness of itself, it chooses to clear out to regenerate itself, that's what it will do. If so it may be that the human race will have to start again on another level of consciousness. Or, if we are able to increase the awareness of consciousness now, then we may be able to be part of the ongoing cleaning, without having to be purged out. But there's nothing to be alarmed about, it's just a natural process of creation.

By contrast Veronica, Nora and Katrine were more optimistic that a widespread clearout is unlikely:

> There have already been instances of a catastrophe that have worked to help the earth towards where it's going. The earth plane is headed towards global catastrophe at the moment, through the change in the earth's atmosphere and the way its resources are being used... There is likely to be another ice age. But that may shift. There are shifts constantly taking place towards that level of catastrophe being unnecessary... So the extent of the clearout depends upon those who are incarnate now, and who will be leading up to that time.

> Changes will be made, and new guidelines will be introduced, because it is not possible to go on otherwise the planet will be destroyed... It's difficult to learn now because there is too much going on, so there are some difficult choices to be made about how to change things on earth but with the least harm... We are working to avoid large-scale catastrophe, although something has to happen to clear out some people, because the population issue is a big problem. So we are trying to work out how to do this, but at the same time keeping the earth itself in place as a learning environment is very important.

> Before civilization was concentrated in smaller places, now it's more spread out. So it's as if we have made this decision to 'go for it', and you can't wipe out the whole human race because you would lose planet earth, and it is much more important that we continue the work we are doing. If humans wipe it out for themselves, so be it, we will find a different place.

But that is not how it is looking right now.

Claire was again unique in adopting the somewhat different tack that the 'end of the experiment' is at hand – irrespective of any choices humanity might make – presumably, if we recall her reports in the previous section, because a collective soul decision has already been made to change the experiment. But she too adopted the view that a wholesale clearout will not be necessary:

> Because the end of the experiment is near, there has to be a thinning of the veil and an expanding awareness of being part of the One... This is going to cause dissatisfaction amongst and discord with those who remain in the old energy, and continue to abuse the planet. But as more people become aware of who they truly are, more of them will become more willing to help the earth repair itself... It is difficult to influence those who choose to forget and don't want to realize the damage they are causing through their greed, and this is why past civilizations chose to end themselves. There has to be some sort of multinational disaster or occurrence of some sort to enable this shift to take place... But it hasn't been finalized, and it won't be a total disaster as in the past... And afterwards, those who remain in the physical will be aware of who they really are, while those souls who choose not to move forward will not reincarnate in the new experiment.

3.4.3 Are our global political systems seriously jeopardizing our spiritual development?

We were originally anticipating that in response to this question our sources would condemn greedy and power-crazed multinationals and politicians. Instead, in line with a more detached view that humanity is collectively responsible for its own mess and cannot blame different factions, Alva pulled us up short by reminding us that our political systems are our own historic, collective creations: 'Any government is only a result of the energy of the souls living there.' Veronica and Amy expanded on a similar theme:

> Ultimately they do not stand in the way, they merely challenge you to look within and see whether this is something that you want enough, or whether you will give in if challenged. Ultimately it is only our incarnate selves that stand in the way.

> Anything that takes away the power of the individual and the community is not a good thing. It's out of balance. You need to bring community back so people know their place and are respected in their society... People first need to change their thinking, to see themselves as part of a

greater whole. If they see themselves as having worth, then they'll pull away from that need to be controlled and organized. And then smaller communities will form, so that people can collectively grow, when they've found their individual power again.

However Alva followed this up by focusing on what appears to be North America as an example. I do not wish to cause specific offence by including her comments, but she subsequently confirmed that these were not her own conscious thoughts by saying 'how this came through I do not know', so I feel that it would be selective to omit them:

> Take America for example. Its people had experienced a lot of pain, hurt, poverty and suffering before they went there. The native people originally had a balanced energy, they lived in harmony with nature and the animals. But the newcomers brought all their old experiences and hate with them, and built a society based on those fears. They didn't know how to handle the good energy that was there from before, and they handled it in the only way they knew. They sort of slaughtered it all, for their own society, based on their fear and need of control. And that's how the whole community is still working.

Alva did add that 'this may also be where the rebalancing will first take place'. Indeed, to provide some additional balance of my own, the British and other empires have been equally guilty of such ignorance in other parts of the world.

These messages caused me to reflect that there is another fundamental reason why we should avoid the human tendency to factionalize and discriminate, and to blame those who do not see things our way for all our problems. It is the blindingly obvious but rarely considered fact that we have *all* contributed to the current state of affairs in our various past incarnations. Any one of us will almost certainly have played our part at some time, as a merciless conqueror, an ambitious politician or a greedy commercial operator. So we would do well to reflect that, just because we may not be in those roles this time around, as souls we are hardly blameless for the way our world has developed.

3.4.4 Are there any major plans to assist humanity's spiritual development? If so, do they involve more evolved souls incarnating, or a lifting of the veil of amnesia?

To balance any perception of undue negativity or detachment in their previous assessments of the state of our planet, our sources consistently suggested that help is at hand to raise the general level of spiritual awareness and connection in the world at large. This is of course a theme that has been prevalent in spiritual and new age circles for many decades, often linked to the dawning of the Age of Aquarius, so there is an increased possibility of conscious interference in this area. But none of this material has been omitted, to allow you to make up your own mind about it.

We will commence with the general responses from David, Denise, Katrine and Alva:

> We are doing this all the time… One plan is to allow more people that are incarnate this level of communication we are involved in now... There will also be an awakening amongst groups of people, and with that knowledge comes responsibility for taking control of their lives.

> Not major plans, but much has been done and put in place already, which will become known naturally at the right time… The determination of the next generation as a whole will have the capacity to build on changes that have been started already.

> Increasingly we are teaching soul groups to specialize in different areas, for example with animals and environmental issues, instead of everybody doing everything... And more souls are coming down now specifically for environmental reasons, to work with the environmental groups all over the world.

> As humans take one step towards the spirit world, just by saying 'help, help me, I need help', that is an invitation and the spiritual masters will be listening. Then they'll know that we are ready to receive guidance, and it will be given to us.

One specific aspect of this, which most of our sources commented on, is that more evolved souls are incarnating to assist with the raising of awareness. David merely reported that there are 'many', but Veronica, Nora and Nadine went further:

> There are many souls working towards raising the awareness, including some souls and groups coming into incarnation now whose sole aim is to do just that… Their purer, more highly evolved energies are needed much more than ever before… They will help to speed up the raising of the earth's vibration by helping others to reach a level of enlightenment, by helping other souls to evolve and develop. By simply being here they raise the energies of the earth.

> Highly evolved souls are being asked to come back, but we need quite a few of them to choose to be a part of it… Many more souls are now working on new insights and knowledge, and bringing it out to as many

people as possible, but it has to speed up. These are souls who have learned all their lessons but are coming back to help others, to learn about the environment, and stop being preoccupied with money and power and only thinking about themselves... There are many different ways of helping people, because everyone is different, so there has to be a wide variety of help.

Awareness is changing, it is going up to another level. And as it does that, the awareness of our connection to the earth will move up another level. There are many healer children present on this earth right now who are at the next stage. The atmosphere is changing to such an extent that frequency levels are getting higher. So these young children who are moving into the world right now are able to absorb this higher energy, which leaves their awareness a little more open than former generations.

Nadine also suggested that some of these souls originate from other planets and dimensions, and Amy, Naomi and Claire supported this view:

They are coming down to lend a hand with the uplifting of energy... Sometimes they are so, so extremely knowledgeable that it's as if they create a spark of light that illuminates conscious awareness. And at the same moment, the planet lights up in that knowledge and slowly people bring it into consciousness.

They have a very specific task... The earth needs new ideas, and new solutions to old problems that they might have dealt with before.

There is a need for a different understanding in the world, both technically and spiritually. It is going to go through a huge change, and you need the expertise... You don't yet have in your hands many of the discoveries that are needed to save you from mass extinction. These more advanced souls who are incarnating will be able to pass on some of that knowledge. And some of them will also be able to pass on different spiritual awareness, and be leaders in that way.

They are incarnating to help those on earth remember who they really are, that they are part of the Source, so that the experiment can change and move to a new energy level. It's part of the shift. There will be a thinning of the veil.

This is the second time that Claire has explicitly referred to a deliberate 'thinning of the veil' in this section, and according to her this is an integral part of the new experiment. Meanwhile Newton's brief report that the veil has been deliberately thickened in the last few thousand years – which I discussed in section 3.2, and which was supported by some of our sources – was accompanied by the suggestion that there is increasing pressure in the light realms for this decision to be at least partially reversed. So, as we might expect, many of our sources suggested that this too is as an integral part of the raising of awareness. Here are Katrine, Alva, Veronica and Amy:

> The veil is getting thinner and thinner. We are teaching souls how to get in touch with their higher part more easily when they are incarnate.

> As humans learn how to 'be' on a soul level, the connection is getting stronger and broader, so they can sort of experience both worlds.

> The veil between the spirit and earth planes can only be fully lifted once a certain level of awareness has been reached by everyone... Many of those who are not open to the spiritual side of their nature would find it too difficult to suddenly be living like that, so it needs to be gradual in order to fully achieve what needs to be achieved.

> We are allowing people to better remember who they are. Bringing heaven to earth, but in a way involving remembering and being in connection with their soul essence in the physical life, so they make more conscious choices about their lives, what they're doing, how they're behaving... That's why people are becoming more psychic, more aware, so that they can start to learn to rebuild the awareness of themselves. Humanity has tried to do this before, and hasn't achieved it. But with this challenge, this time, more people are more aware. Communications have assisted with the ability to transmit information, whereas in times past that network wasn't in place. So more people can access the awareness and the knowledge. And the souls that have a raised frequency will affect all the ones that don't, and help to pull them up.

Despite these encouraging reports, we should be clear that there is likely to be a rider on any deliberate policy to thin the veil. As Nora pointed out: 'Although the veil becomes less and less as we evolve anyway, it is difficult to learn human lessons if we know everything at the beginning.' Moreover, we know that many of our sources continue to regard earth as providing a relatively unique learning experience, which at least in part derives from it being a dense and emotional experience that involves making free choices – without prior knowledge of our life plans. So if the experiment is to change once again, I would suggest that there can only be a partial lifting of the veil – just sufficient to make us more automatically aware of our true spiritual nature, without knowing all the answers in advance. Nevertheless, it is certainly possible that there is a collective soul agreement that humanity has now learned enough from the imposition of a thickened veil, and cannot now progress properly without it being at least partially thinned.

Newton's subjects have also reported that souls are able to take more of their soul energy into incarnation in other less physical, easier worlds, and in *The Book of the Soul* I tentatively suggested that this was why they retained a higher degree of soul awareness on them. So it may be that the current lifting of the veil on earth will involve being able to bring a larger proportion of our soul energy into incarnation without 'blowing our circuits'. However we should remember that, because of the holographic nature of soul energy, and because of the way it is constantly recycled back to the Source, it is not only the quantity of energy we bring down that matters but also its quality and concentration – which should increase naturally over time anyway. This may be what Alva was hinting at when she reported that 'now we bring more and more, yet at the same time less and less, because we don't need so much'.

In conclusion, the general idea from all our sources seems to be that there is a shift of consciousness taking place on earth – involving what is probably a gradual reversal of a former decision – whereby our level of spiritual amnesia is being reduced, accompanied by the incarnation of more evolved souls. Nevertheless there is also support for the message I put forward in *Genesis Unveiled* that, as before, we may be heading for an at least partially global catastrophe as the only way to initiate a major transformation – although this time it would involve global warming, and be of our own making. But this is not guaranteed. Ultimately the strongest message seems to be that our fate is in our own hands – both at a human and a soul level.

4

REALITY AND TIME

Our fourth group of questions deals with more strictly philosophical and scientific topics, including the notions that we create our own reality and that time does not really exist. They take us into territory that is arguably *the* most complex for our limited human perspective to understand. And because of this we will find that broader elements of discussion and analysis that add to our sources' comments are particularly useful in this chapter.

Creating Our Own Reality

4.1 Do we create our own reality by the power of our thoughts and intentions?

Modern lifestyle gurus have written numerous books based around the simple but important premise of 'positive thinking', so the idea that our thoughts and intentions create the psychic undercurrents that determine the events in our lives is not a new one. It therefore came as no surprise that a number of our sources backed the proposition that we create our own reality. David's brief reply was 'every minute of every day', but Veronica and Nadine were more forthcoming:

> To a very large extent. Energy follows thoughts and intentions, so the more we think about something, the more likely it is to happen. We attract things by sending out energy... So do whatever you want, think whatever you want, as long as it harms no one... Every word and every thought has an effect at some level.

> We do it every day. You can create any number of outcomes just through your thought patterns, and what you experience are the outcomes that you may have intentionally or unintentionally put into place.

When Andy followed up by asking if our thoughts were the most important element, Nadine's independence and objectivity came to the fore:

> No, it's controlling your *intentions* that is important. Intention comes before thought... If I had an intention to create a particular outcome, I'd have a feeling that I needed to do something, and that intent would create itself into a thought of what exactly it was I needed to do. Then as I express what I'm thinking I give it a form in terms of how I see that image. And if I choose to write it down then it becomes a little more concrete. And if I choose to act upon it then that thought-form has now become an act of creation. It becomes more a form of matter that is manifested in front of me. That happens on every level of your energetic form, whether it's emotional, mental or spiritual.

So far so good. But this idea that we create our own reality tends to be tied into the ancient esoteric notion that the physical world is entirely an illusion, which is now supposedly reinforced by modern scientific research into quantum theory. This is a complex and controversial area that is discussed in far more detail in a paper on my website. But the crucial point for the discussion at hand is that we should perhaps be wary of oversimplification when there is so much professional disagreement among theorists about how best to *interpret* basic quantum theory. Indeed, it appears that the linkages made by some of them between what happens in the quantum world and what happens in the macroscopic world of complex systems – that is, at the level of human experience – may have been somewhat overstated.

Moreover the whole issue of the physical world being an illusion is itself fraught with controversy. For example, when we ride a motorbike into a brick wall we tend to experience the physicality of matter to pretty devastating effect – and it seems unlikely that even the most highly trained, nail-bed-lying, coal-walking, brick-smashing adept would walk away completely unscathed from such an encounter. In fact it increasingly looks as if modern consciousness research, not quantum theory, will prove to be of most use in refining a modern spiritual worldview.

Meanwhile it would appear that, apart from there being certain genuinely physical constraints on our ability to create our own reality, there are two further constraints that are not discussed by spiritually oriented quantum theorists, as we are about to find out.

4.1.1 Why do we not always achieve the outcomes we desire?

There is a paradox that is clearly expressed in two exhortations that we regularly use on our children. On the one hand we tell them that 'anything is possible if you want it enough'. On the other hand we prepare them for failure by insisting that 'we do not always get what we want'. So which is true? Can clear intent, positive thinking and focused visualization fulfill our every dream or not? The answer, according to our sources, is 'sometimes'.

Naomi simply replied that 'a person may wish to go in one direction, but their karma may choose for them to go in another because there are issues that have to be addressed'. But Nora, Denise and Katrine provided the following information when answering the primary question alone and without further prompting:

> Sometimes we think we create our reality more than we actually do. Especially when we are moving away from the lesson we are meant to be learning, we let our thoughts almost block out the thing we are supposed to be doing and we start doing other things. And then we have to go back and do it again. So if we let things happen without thinking too much we usually learn quicker and the right things will happen – although we can always choose different details of how to work within that lesson, as long as we don't move too far away from it… Sometimes if a soul's lesson is to be poor and lonely, they will not get riches or companionship no matter how much they focus on them. Sometimes they may be able to fulfill such desires at least in part, or for a little while, but they will be taken away again.

> Good intentions that are purely focused are very strong and powerful. But too many people allow doubt and fear in… They become distracted from their plan because the human aspect becomes stronger than the soul aspect, and this produces a negative spiral and attracts more turmoil and emotion and fear and doubt. As this happens the focus and strength of the original, pure intent becomes weaker, and the path of the soul becomes longer and more difficult.

> When we think positively it will affect our lives. It may not be in the way we expect, but it will be the best result… As humans we don't know what is best for us anyway. Humans sometimes misunderstand, they may think that what's happening is not for the best, and they then get caught up in that and it's like being trapped… They don't see the other things happening that are helping their positive desires to come to fruition in another way, and they focus too much on their own solution. So they might think positively about something in their life that they want, and it

doesn't happen, but then something else happens that is better – because they didn't know that what they wanted was not the best thing for them, and the other thing happens to make up for that. But if you don't open up and see the whole picture you might even miss the other good thing that is happening... For example, if you want a loving partner in your life, something else might happen like a positive change in your living situation or a new friend comes along, so that you'll have love in your life in a different way. But if you are too fixated on your original intent you may miss this other opportunity.

They were clearly united in the view that, although we have free will, there are sometimes spiritual forces at work behind the scenes to keep us on our chosen life paths. This despite the fact that most of the time we are not aware of their efforts – and indeed, with our lack of soul perspective, may even be rather less than appreciative of them. Katrine also confirmed Andy's suggestion that it is spirit guides and other helpers who perform this role, adding: 'They do this a lot, because they have a greater understanding of what you need, rather than what you ask for based on what you think you need. But they will help you more if you talk to them.'

4.1.2 Can interaction with other people's life plans or intentions restrict this ability?

Before we look at what our sources had to say in response to this question, it will be useful to recap a little background theory. One of the implications of the idea that the physical world is an illusion is that everything we perceive around us is the result of our subjective conditioning. To a significant extent this is true, although again any linkage between this and quantum theory may tend to be overstated. However it appears that those who put forward this view are missing a vital element of the picture, perhaps in part because they tend to be drawn towards the notion of soul unity rather than recognizing the idea of the Holographic Soul as representing unity and individuality at the same time. But this latter suggests there is at least one element of physical reality that is *not* merely subjective – and that is our *interactions* with the incarnate consciousness of *other souls*. If we limit this to the human level for simplicity, it is clear that – however subjective our perceptions of our physical surroundings might be – at a fundamental level we are interactively involved in creating a reality that is shared.

It is this proposition that we are involved in a unique, *collectively created* physical reality – not in the automatic sense that we are all aspects of the Source, but as interacting, individual soul consciousnesses – that most spiritually oriented quantum theorists do not seem to appreciate. Moreover it is not expressed in *The Book of the Soul*, merely in a subsequent paper on my website. In any case, the majority of our subjects subsequently reported that they had little knowledge of or interest in the topics discussed in this group of questions prior to their sessions. It is therefore of vital importance that our sources should have consistently corroborated this crucial idea, not so much in direct answer to this question but because it underlies their responses throughout this chapter.

The idea of a collectively created physical reality is most obviously in evidence when two individuals have such directly conflicting immediate desires that only one of them can achieve their aim. For example, when two politicians are directly vying for a specific post, clearly only one of them can be elected at any one time. Katrine hinted at this constraint when she said 'of course our own thoughts and actions will affect those around us too', while Alva agreed with Andy's suggestion that there is a significant interaction between our own intentions and those of others. But Amy was the only source who focused directly on this particular issue, which she did in response to the primary question and without further prompting:

> They are really glad you asked that, because they see that people are struggling with that question. You have chosen the lifetime you've gone into, and you've chosen the events that happen, the people you are going to meet and the work you are going to do. Part of your collective learning is about the unconscious mind and how it controls your living experience, and how your soul and your unconscious mind work hand in hand and together create the physical reality you live in. Your soul knows the lessons you have come to learn, and the better connection your soul has with your unconscious personality-mind the better chance you have of learning them, and of creating the reality that you've already chosen. So it's a constant communication on that level. Sometimes if you're on a particular track and your soul thinks 'hang on, this isn't working', it works with your unconscious mind to create the right ingredients to get you where you need to be. And even though you've chosen your life plan, other people's free will can get in the way and create an obstacle.
> *Can you talk about this interaction in more detail?*
> Everything is part of an overall plan. Nothing is wasted, and nothing goes astray that much.
> *What if someone else deviates from their planned interactions with you?*
> Part of our challenge is to work out how to react to keep things on track.

There are contingency plans for the key choice points, and you can always find a way around things, it's all part of the learning process. But the overall plan is always there, and everything is watched and noticed.

So what practical, spiritual advice emerges from all this? On an individual level there can be little doubt that positive thinking is an extremely powerful tool, especially when combined with the right intentions and felt consistently with every part of our being – and not just as a fleeting thought superimposed on a broad canvas of conventional doubt and lethargy. Furthermore, if the desired outcome of that thinking is broadly in line with our life plan, it will usually come about. However it will not necessarily be in the manner, or at the time, that we expect. So the lesson from our sources seems to be that our best chance of keeping on track with our plan, and of growing in the way that we intended, is to keep an open connection to our higher self and our spirit guide. Nor, it seems, should we attempt to be too specific about what we wish for, or that it should happen in the short-term. That way lies sufficient possible disenchantment that it can act as a block on the other important events that *are* actually meant to be happening in our lives – or at least we may not pay them the attention they deserve. The key is to *flow* with the apparently good and bad, the apparently lucky and unlucky, the apparent successes and failures, and to *trust* that if we remain open and connected we will not stray far from the path we have set for ourselves. We should strive to remain *relaxed*, but alert to synchronicities and intuitive promptings. Indeed, having reinforced our long-term intent if we feel sufficiently sure that our intuition about it is correct, we should just focus on 'the now', and everything we can do *now* to make that intent come to fruition. That way we divest ourselves of all baggage both from the past and from the potential future.

Conscious Co-Creation

Claire's response to the above question was revealing: 'Individuals have some power to affect their reality. But the more there are, and if there is consensus between many souls, the stronger the effect.' In fact she regularly referred to the idea of 'conscious co-creation' in her research session. For example, when discussing whether or not the earth plane is unique in section 2.6 she reported that 'the physical reality of earth is unique at the present time in so far as there is no conscious creation'. Then when discussing how evolved souls from other realms are coming down to assist the shift in consciousness in section 3.4, she asserted that 'they are helping those on earth to become conscious creators of this reality'. She also mentioned it in section 3.2 as a quality seemingly possessed by the Lemurians and to a lesser extent the Atlanteans, even though she had little prior knowledge of the spiritual aspect of these civilizations. So even though she subsequently indicated that she had spent time learning about ways of creating your own reality as an individual and even in small groups, it does seem possible that her descriptions of this rather broader process were not merely regurgitations of prior knowledge.

Denise too made some further comments that seem to support this idea, and she confirmed subsequently that it was entirely new to her:

> Souls can experience many things, and there's some sort of an understanding, although we've not reached that point yet, that humanity's purpose is to become so in tune with the Oneness, with that feeling of such purity – it's hard to put into words what that feeling is like – that they evolve the world that they want to experience.

So although these reports come from just two sources, it seems clear that they cannot be summarily dismissed on the grounds of prior knowledge and conscious interference. To the extent that they might represent genuine information from separate sources, my interpretation of them is as follows. In conjunction with a possible lowering of the veil, they seem to refer to our actions and awareness in the physical rather than to any idea of collective soul intent exercised in the light realms, albeit that the two cannot be entirely separated. The idea seems to be that we should switch our perspective away from the spiritually *unconscious* co-creation that manifests in collectively *conflicting* desires, and onto the possibilities that might unfold if we were to attempt to *consciously* co-create our reality by exerting our spiritual focus with *united* intent.

There can be no doubt that this scenario is the closest we could come to 'heaven on earth', and because of its importance it is worth us taking a few moments to discuss it further. So is it a realistic possibility in the face of a widespread agenda of materialism, planetary destruction and cultural breakdown? Can groups of people really come together and attempt to consciously and deliberately influence events for the better as a collaborative, consensual, spiritual exercise? One man has arguably done more than any other to lay some groundwork that suggests that maybe, just maybe, we can.

John Hagelin is a quantum physicist by training, but whether or not quantum rather than consciousness theory provides the underlying explanation for his research findings is of only secondary importance here. In the summer of 1993 he initiated an experiment to see if the collective use of Transcendental Meditation could reduce violent crime in Washington DC. Volunteers came from all over the globe, their numbers swelling from around 500 at the start to nearly 4000 by the end of eight weeks. The result was a demonstrable reduction in violent crime of nearly 25 percent over the period in question. Moreover, despite the predictably simplistic, reductionist and selective attempts by a few hardened skeptics at debunking this experiment, it is clear that the statistical analysis was carried out according to the highest professional standards and in cooperation with the police force's own statisticians. For example, it used time-series analysis to rule out a long list of alternative explanations, including weather variables, seasonal effects, changes in police surveillance, and other trends and cyclical patterns inherent in the crime data.

Hagelin has since gone on to create a framework for volunteers who are trained in Transcendental Meditation to come together as 'peace-creating experts' in any part of the world. Admittedly the spiritual framework that underlies this essentially Vedic movement may not be totally consistent with the worldview I propose. In addition, rather than focusing on a specific outcome, the meditation technique used involves attaining a general transcendental state that is intended to cause waves of tranquility, unity and love to ripple out into the surroundings. Nevertheless, I would suggest that Hagelin's efforts should be applauded and supported.

The Nature of Time and Parallel Dimensions

4.2 Can you explain how the notion of time really works?

Much esoteric thinking holds that not only is the physical world an illusion, but also the notion of time that tends to be associated with it. So what did our sources have to say on the matter?

As we have seen at various times previously, they were unanimous that time is a concept that only has relevance in the physical plane. However, instead of belittling humanity for not being sufficiently advanced to see through the illusion of time as some spiritual commentators might suggest, they all agreed that this is a deliberately designed aspect of the physical plane, which is necessary for us to be able to grow and experience when incarnate. Indeed so consistent are their answers that there is a fair degree of repetition, but each one contains elements that are not so obvious that anyone could have come up with them. So the key points from each are presented, again in the hope of demonstrating the high probability that they came from our sources themselves – especially when we remember that our subjects all subsequently professed a conscious lack of interest in the topic at hand. Here are, in order, Denise, David, Veronica, Nadine, Nora, Naomi, Katrine, Claire, Amy and Alva:

Time in the earth plane is there to help you to live a human life, to regulate and order it.

It's necessary to maintain the illusion of time, at least on earth... It would be too complicated for humans to realize that past, present and future are all one. It's enough for most humans just to deal with their current life.

On the earth plane time gives humanity a framework to work in. It allows us to look at things that have happened, and plan towards things that will happen. Without it there would be confusion... But as souls there is no end, no beginning, no past, no present, no future.

Time exists on the earth plane because it's a construct of the human mind, in order to make sense of what's gone on behind them and what's going on in front of them. But it doesn't really exist. All time is now. We are now. Also time on the earthly plane is slower because of the heaviness and denseness of matter, so time too, because it's wrapped up in space pulled down onto this plane, has a very slow frequency. It is pulled out or drawn out. So it feels like it gives us that linear sense. But if you were to take it up to the higher levels, it goes, it's insubstantial.

It's complicated. As earth beings time allows you to be able to cope by remembering what you have done in the past and the options you can look forward to in the future. But up here time doesn't matter as much. Someone can go off for a life and seem to be back again only the next moment, even though they have had a full lifetime on earth.

Time is only of relevance outside the spiritual world. There is no time in the spiritual world. The future, present and past all happen at the same time. It's a hard concept to understand. In the physical world, time is necessary so one can learn. If you don't have time it is not possible to understand what one did in the past and to improve.

There is no time, only the illusion of time because humans could not cope otherwise... Humans need concepts of past, present and future, but in the soul realms we don't live like that. We don't use time as a basis for anything, because it signifies nothing to us.

Linear time came into being because anything in physical form needs it to be able to exist, in order to change. The concept of no time is impossible to understand in physical form, it can't be explained... But for the soul the differences between past, present and future are not so apparent.

Earth needs a timeline as part of its development, as a way of ordering things, but here in the spirit world time is just constant, it's everywhere, it's everything. It's as if you can look down from a layer where time just doesn't exist, or is everywhere at once, onto a lower level where there is a definite progression from past to future. But it's also a way of gauging a soul's development, it's a way of making concrete the experiences that a soul can attain, and the same is true of other physical places.

Time is part of the physical experience... Without it we wouldn't understand, because we experience our physical existence via the physical brain... We learn what light is only by experiencing its opposite, darkness. By the same token, it is only by being set into a physical form with time limitations that we can learn what it is to be completely free from that... In the spirit realms, the only thing that matters is how much experience your soul has obtained from all kinds of lifeforms... There is only the yearning to be complete.

So time is essential to our experience of the physical plane. But what about the light realms? All of our sources suggest that here time is meaningless. Yet we saw in the Introduction that interlife regression subjects at least to some extent experience a timeline of consecutive events, with a degree of cause and effect, even if they are aware that their perceptions of *elapsed* time are totally different. And the solution to this conundrum seems to be that although genuine soul experience in the light realms is timeless, and has the qualities of an eternal now, when it is recalled in the physical plane under regression it is at least partially imbued with a timeline so that we can understand and learn from it. Indeed, this seems to confirm that it is pretty much impossible for our limited human perceptions to appreciate the true nature of this fundamental reality with no time, even if we have all experienced it before and will do so again on our return to the light realms. All we can do, perhaps, is glimpse it, along with the associated perception that we are all One, during transcendental and enlightenment episodes when in altered states of consciousness.

However this leads us into an even worse conundrum because, if there is fundamentally no time in the light realms, then how can souls vary in experience? Indeed how can the whole learning, experience and growth model work at all? This question seems almost impossible to answer in any concrete and infallible way. All one can suggest is that the apparent absence of time *as we know it* in the light realms does not prevent some sense of continuity and of cause and effect being maintained within them.

4.2.1 Are there multiple, physical, earth realities all playing out in parallel?

Before we look at what our sources had to say in response to this question, again it will be useful to recap a little background theory. We have already seen that there are many other dimensions or 'realities' in which we can gain experience. However supporters of the 'many worlds interpretation' of modern quantum theory suggest that there are multiple, physical, *earth* realities, with each one playing out in parallel but largely independently so that our soul consciousness is only aware of one at a time. This is an alternative to the more conventional interpretation that the quantum wave function collapses during observation, but it still has many supporters – not least in the science-fiction community.

So does this proposition even have any theoretical validity? Apart from the fact that it remains unproven from a scientific perspective, some of its more spiritually oriented supporters suggest that a parallel world is only created when, for example, a human consciousness faces a major decision that has several outcomes. From this they argue that only a limited number of parallel worlds would be created. However their attempts to limit the theory in this way make no associated attempt to identify what would constitute a major decision – understandably, because who would dare to try to define something so nebulous and personal? By contrast, it seems that a more strictly mathematical and philosophically logical application of the many worlds interpretation would insist that a parallel world is created for every single possible outcome at the quantum level – which would, of course, mean that a virtually infinite number of parallel worlds would be created at every instant.

What implications would this theory have from a soul perspective? The key issue is that our soul consciousness would somehow have to be involved in an infinite number of parallel worlds, not just a couple in which portions of our soul energy could perhaps have concurrent incarnations and then reunite in the light realms. Given its holographic nature it may well be possible for soul consciousness to diversify into infinity in this way. But would the individual soul aspects ever be 'reunited' with each other, or would each one effectively represent a new, separate soul identity? Some theorists argue that parallel worlds might remerge if they were somehow limited to maintaining certain internal consistencies in terms of time and the number of people affected, but again these attempts at limitation seem somewhat illogical and poorly defined. So if there were no limitations, we have to ask what point would be served by so much effort being put into learning from an infinite number of experiences, most of which would be only minutely differentiated? Many people regard the multiple worlds interpretation as having great philosophical and scientific 'elegance' – the definition of which is a simple theory that is able to explain many different phenomena. However, viewed from a spiritual perspective that accepts the genuinely holographic rather than purely unitary nature of soul consciousness, arguably it becomes decidedly inelegant and cumbersome.

So what did our sources have to say? Unfortunately it took some time for us to phrase this question carefully enough to ensure that they did not go off on a tangent and talk about other more general realities, whether physical or not. So we only have limited direct answers to this question proper. But the three that did answer it, that is Amy, Nora and Naomi, were all emphatic that there is only one physical reality – although unusually the latter two added the rider 'as far as I am aware', which suggests that on this occasion they were tackling a difficult issue from only a limited soul perspective.

Nevertheless, there is another aspect of our research that has a fundamental bearing on this issue. In section 1.6 our sources were adamant that the reliving of experiences in the light realms, even to the extent of soul memory sharing, does not have the same qualities as the original experience in the physical plane. Here is Katrine picking up on this difference again:

> Only as a soul can you go to different timelines or lives and experience them. It's like movies playing at the same time and you can choose which one you want to watch. But it's not really physical in the way you experience this life, it's just experienced as physical.

There can surely be little doubt that the major reason soul memories do not have the same qualities as the original experience in the physical plane is because the latter is a collectively created, shared, interactive experience – and as such represents a single, unique, physical reality. This is completely at odds with the idea of multiple parallel realities, under which model every experience would be indistinguishable. Indeed the latter theory appears not to have been properly thought through from a spiritual perspective at all. But to the extent that it can be, it would probably have to fall back on the assumption that soul unity reigns supreme, while any notion of soul individuality is illusory – which would again fail to take account of the true holographic nature of soul consciousness.

4.2.2 Can we go back in time and alter events?

Again we will need to cover a little background before we let our sources speak on this subject. We have already seen in the Introduction that in the light realms souls can go back and replay or even role-play events from any of their past lives, as well as being able to experience the past lives of others. So it is clear that at this fundamental level we can experience these lives again on an individual, or even group, basis – and when we do they may well appear just as real as when they originally happened, just as they can for past-life regression subjects. To this extent any lives in the 'past' are still available to be played out in the 'present'. But it also seems clear that no amount of role-playing in these experiences can alter the unique, original, physical reality that we interactively and collectively created.

Nevertheless, the idea that science-fiction writers and aficionados have so enthusiastically embraced is that it might be possible to travel back in time and alter events in the *physical* plane, even though there seems to be little doubt that most of their attempts to portray this in books and films have been entirely lacking in scientific logic and consistency. But one of the major reasons that some quantum theorists support the multiple worlds interpretation is precisely because it allows them to overcome some of the paradoxes that beset the notion of time travel – like, for example, the traveler going back and killing one of their parents before they were conceived. So they suggest that at some stage wormholes could be used to travel backwards and that, if events were altered that would normally cause an irresolvable paradox, these would then be played out in a parallel world.

We have already seen that this idea of parallel worlds has fundamental flaws and was rejected by those of our sources who commented usefully on it. So it will come as no surprise that the similarly few who commented usefully on the notion of time travel in the physical rejected that as well, thereby supporting the majority of hard-headed theoretical physicists. Naomi again emphasized that it is only possible to revisit the past in the light realms, and that as a result this experience can only have an impact on the soul concerned:

> If a soul goes back to a past life it will affect that soul's experience and emotional make-up only... So if a warmonger went back to his life, he would not be able to affect the outcome of what he did, but he could change his emotional outlook about what he did. So rather than die loathing his enemies he could understand the grievous wrongs he had done them, and that instant thought process would change his next life.

Meanwhile Andy asked Katrine whether souls can actually choose to reincarnate in earth's past, and her dismissive response was 'that would be pointless'. When he put the same question to Amy, she was even more dismissive on behalf of her sources:

> What would be the use of that? They're leaving that up to you to answer.
> *Perhaps to experience something that couldn't be experienced now.*
> They're saying that you can experience all time from wherever you are, you don't have to go back into physical time to experience it, because the memories, the echoes, the layers of time, they're all still with you. There is also a progression of cultural development, and we're all part of that forward movement in earth, physical terms. So to go back and forward would not be beneficial for development.
> *So souls only incarnate in the present?*
> Exactly. Because the consciousness of humanity as a whole has to be moving in the same direction.

4.2.3 Are our individual futures already known?

Throughout this book the supremacy of individual choice, personal responsibility and free will has been emphasized. For this reason it appears that the future only exists in the 'now' as a set of major probabilities and lesser possibilities. So when souls preview their next lives the details of these are only *envisaged*, and have not yet been realized or made manifest, and collectively and interactively *experienced* in the physical plane. How closely they will mirror the versions we glimpsed before birth will depend entirely on the incarnate choices made by all the key players. Nevertheless we specifically wanted to know what our sources would make of the issue of predetermination versus free will.

Unsurprisingly David and Nadine confirmed that the future is not predetermined specifically by comparing life previews in the light realms with the physical reality of earth:

> When we are previewing a life we are aware that we are only involved with that life rather than living it... The future is never fixed, there is

nothing that is certain, because of free will.

In the spiritual plane you can glimpse parts of your future, but you cannot see the details until they've actually been experienced... Because there is free will, there are infinite potentials that can actually be.

Claire and Amy seemed to support this view, this time when asked by Andy if it is possible to predict the future while in the physical plane:

At any one moment in present time, for those who are gifted, it is possible to obtain ideas of possible futures, although some are more probable than others... They are subject to change because they have not been realized by many.

Again, they're saying what would be the use of that? Where you are now as a soul is where you have developed to, with all the learnings, so jumping ahead serves no purpose. And it can sometimes be a fabrication. You can look at your choices for the current life, and the important crossover points, but you can't look ahead to another life because you haven't learned what this one is about yet. And the future lessons depend on the lessons that are learned now.

Meanwhile Alva took the view that the future is happening now, even if her other comments were somewhat more enigmatic:

The future's not future, it's now... But any view of the future will always be filtered through that person's soul and experience, and must always be understood from that point of view.

Naomi also picked up on the apparent paradox of concurrent lives as it appears to our human perceptions:

All lives are led at the same time. Despite this, the future ones can change. That is just how it is, and I probably can't explain it any better.

Let us briefly examine this idea of concurrent lives in more detail. More than anything else the concept of a 'life' itself requires the concept of time, because it clearly has a start, middle and end. So this suggestion, which relies intrinsically on the concept of time, must itself be meaningless – *unless* it is placed strictly in the context of the physical plane. But the one collectively created physical reality is governed by standard notions of linear time, and for very good reason. So if we view these issues from a strictly human perspective, which is the only way we can make any real sense of them while incarnate, then it surely remains reasonable to view our lives as happening consecutively rather than concurrently.

Again, we might ask what are the practical implications of all this? The first point we can make is that it appears that there is no useful sense in which the future is already happening and can influence the past, despite what appear to be the rather misguided attempts of a few therapists to *progress* their subjects into their possible futures. So it appears we are far better employed concentrating on the present, as Nadine points out:

> It's the understanding of *now* that is most important, because that is your future. If you understand that *now* affects your earthly linear future, then you're able to act accordingly in your experience of the now, in order to gain the outcome.

Moreover we cannot leave this topic without discussing the issue of clairvoyant mediums. Katrine had this to say:

> We can look into the future, but usually it does more harm than good... People who call themselves psychics only see one of many possible futures, because of free will. Sometimes they see the most probable outcome for a person on that day, but it might be completely different on another occasion.

When Andy then pressed her on the problem of 'self-fulfilling prophecy' she provided a pretty convincing and forceful condemnation:

> The trouble is that they get so caught up in thinking about the prediction, and that it is going to happen, that they make all their choices based on it – and help it to happen anyway. And then they think that must have been what was supposed to happen all along... When they fixate on it like that they ignore all other possibilities, and that's the real danger... We wish things were different, and we must teach people that it's not always best to try to find out about the future.

Katrine concluded by confirming the importance of concentrating on the present:

> It's important to remember that you help someone most by telling them about their abilities as a soul, and how they can change their way of looking at things *now*, or how they might react differently in certain situations *now*. This is how you help them to go further and get different outcomes, not by telling them about specific people or places in the future.

4.2.4 Is our collective future already known?

Let us now turn our attention to predictions about our collective rather than individual futures. In *The Book of the Soul* I adopted the view that individual free will is so much the dominant factor that our collective future must change hugely from moment to moment. As a result I was somewhat skeptical of attempts by certain pioneers and other supposed seers to predict the global future. But Katrine's response suggests this may have been somewhat hasty:

> Global predictions are supposed to wake people up, to give them more awareness of what can actually happen. For example, even if they see what they're doing to the planet, they don't really understand... These do tend to be more probable than possible outcomes because all the energies are involved together.

Veronica, Nora and Naomi all seemed to support this impression that the 'big picture' is far more probable and predictable than any individual contributions to it, which is why at least in one sense our individual journeys are far more important than the collective destination:

> The bigger picture, the general outline of the future is known... It is the choices we make *now*, the path we're following *now*, the actions we take *now* that are important, not the destination. That's there, that's in place. So it's how we act on our way that matters.

> The big plan was already decided ages ago, so there are some big things that really do have to happen. But the details of how we get there are not decided as long as we stay within the big plan.

> It is one of the paradoxes that the future will be as it will be, but every single day of every single life changes based on the soul's decisions.

Meanwhile Amy added further details:

What about people who attempt to predict future events?
They only pick up probabilities, on a global not a personal level.
Where does that information come from?
It is implanted into the mind of certain people who are chosen because they have the right mental capacity to bring it in with as little corruption as possible. But they are generally given only possibilities, not absolutes. You can't give absolutes because free will is in play. They are usually saying 'if humanity continues with this thread of its development, this is what could happen'. It is like a warning, and the collective souls involved can either heed that warning or not. But it doesn't make it any more probable.
But at a high level, an overall plan is in place?
Yes.
And is this something that you elders have access to?

The elders work on a certain level, they get part of the information. There are others higher up who control and direct that plan, and the elders work with groups to control part of it. It's a little bit like a shepherd and his flock, keeping them going in a particular direction, but there are other shepherds and other flocks, and they are all trying to get to the same point.

Of course what none of this makes clear is exactly what big picture or overall plan we are talking about. We can guess at various levels of objective. For example on a universal level we might assume that, if the Hindu model discussed in section 2.3 is correct, the ultimate plan is for every soul aspect on every plane to gain all useful experience and reunite with the Source. Meanwhile, on a more geocentric level, presumably there will come a time when, as the human race, we will have fulfilled our share of experience collecting on earth – if we do not destroy ourselves first.

But it also seems likely that from the shorter-term earth perspective there will be various 'collective plans' in place at any one time in the light realms, and they represent 'destinations' that are more or less guaranteed depending on their perceived importance and scale. This might appear to contradict the prevalent idea in section 3.4 that humanity has its own collective free will. But, as with all things, this is clearly not a black-and-white area. For example, if collective decisions are made in the light realms by souls who are either still reincarnating on earth, or at least retain a close connection with and interest in it, can these really be said to be 'external' interventions? We should also remember that the more we become conscious co-creators in the physical plane, the less will be the need for any intervention from the light realms.

Of course, this idea of collective plans might also seem to contradict the more general idea of individual free will. But there is a solution to this apparent dichotomy. Free will is the major precondition for us to be able to learn and grow, both while we are incarnate and discarnate. But what about altruistic lives? These are not designed to provide a learning experience for the soul involved, but for those around them, or even for humanity as a whole. So in these lives the soul's normal ability to exercise free will can be deliberately constrained by their prior consent, thereby ensuring that their life is to all intents and purposes predetermined. And presumably if this were true of enough people, a major plan designed and agreed in the light realms could be pretty much guaranteed to be enacted.

To summarize this final section, it is perfectly possible that anything our sources had to say on the complex issues of time and parallel dimensions may have been distorted and compromised by our subjects' human limitations in transmitting it, or by my own interpretations of it. But to the extent that a clear picture emerges, the main conclusions can be restated as follows:

- There is only one unique, collectively created, physical reality. It is deliberately designed so that our human consciousness perceives it via a single timeline with a past, present and future. This is crucial to our ability to learn and grow by experience.

- We cannot go back and alter the collective, physical experience of the past on our own, although on a soul level we can replay or even change events to alter our *perceptions* of them as individuals or small groups.

- The future of the collective experience does not already exist, except as a set of greater probabilities and lesser possibilities that can be previewed on a soul level, because none of these have yet been realized by individual soul choices and free interactions in the physical plane.

- Although time does not exist in the light realms, human perceptions of interlife experiences under regression tend to retain a timeline of sorts so that they can be understood.

5

CONCLUDING QUESTIONS

This last chapter begins with two concluding questions about the research itself – concerning possible conscious interference and variations in answers – which Andy put to our sources at the end of each session. We will then turn to our subjects' general post-session feedback, and move on to some conclusions and summaries of my own, before closing by returning to our sources and their inspiring final messages.

Possible Conscious Interference

5.1 How can we tell if the subject's conscious knowledge is interfering with this research process?

I indicated in the Introduction that one of the key factors in my decision about what extracts to publish was if I felt the subject's conscious mind was interfering at any time. We also discussed how hypnotherapists have a variety of techniques for gauging the depth of a subject's trance, which are discussed in Appendix I, and how Andy was doing everything he could to keep them at the right level – although this could never be totally infallible. As a result we wanted to know if our sources would have anything to say about this issue that might help us.

In fact most of them merely stated 'you will know'. But Alva, Naomi, Nora and Amy expanded as follows:

By intuitively sensing the energy in the answers.

You will know intuitively. Part of the process is that it is up to you to decide if the information you are getting feels right.

The energy will be different. If you are meant to notice the difference, if you have learned to do that intuitively, you will pick it up.

There would be a sense of dissonance, or a lack of resonance. The information might originally be correct, but it might be colored by the subject's perceptions if there was mental resistance or interference.

And this is indeed how it proved to be. With some subjects we had few reservations about any stage of their session. But with some others – in addition to any initial impression Andy might have obtained during the sessions – the more I listened to the recordings and read through the transcripts, the more I found it was possible to tune in and feel whether conscious interference was either more or less likely. The clues lay in the tone of voice, the speed of delivery, and the content and phrasing of the answers. And with experience it became easy to spot that sometimes high-quality information was flowing freely, while at other times answers were more stilted, hesitant, confused or brief – even within one session with one subject.

Meanwhile a variety of other factors also had to be considered relating to prior knowledge and possible conscious interference, and these are discussed in Appendix I.

Variations in Answers

5.2 What are the possible reasons for us obtaining conflicting answers from different subjects?

We have seen that a large number of especially primary and early questions were relatively simple, and that a clear majority opinion soon formed. By contrast, with certain of the rather more complex and involved questions the spread of answers tended to be more varied. We surmised in advance that the main reason why this might occur would be that different subjects have different levels and areas of both soul and physical experience, so their answers might be constrained or even distorted as a result. And this assumption was borne out when we put this issue to our sources. This is what Alva, Naomi, Nora, Denise, Claire, Amy and Veronica had to say:

> The answer is given through the filter of the person answering... The spirits of light can only pass information through the person you are working with, on the level that they are at.

> Different souls will have different levels of information and knowledge. It's also not possible for a soul to receive information that it is not ready for, and that would change its learning process.

Different souls know different things. Some things we know for sure from our own experience. Other things we may have only heard other souls talking about, and we might not have heard it correctly, or they might have been guessing themselves.

Subjects can only answer based on what their soul knows. There are levels.

There are so many different levels of experience, and everything has to go through the understanding of the subject... And the limitation of language is paramount, because it's often like having to answer with a simile.

Your answers will depend on the people you are working with... And there can be a lack of understanding of how to translate spiritual information into understandable, human-level thinking.

There are some things that the host is not ready for, or would find too difficult to comprehend when their consciousness is being used to pass on information.

We also considered whether the different sources *themselves* might have different levels of experience and knowledge, or different views about what the world was ready for, or different ideas about how complex topics should be explained. And Alva, Veronica and Katrine again bore this out:

They have different aspects of understanding.

In soul form there are different perceptions and understandings. There are different personalities just as there are on earth, and some may see things slightly different to others. There are also some things that some may feel it is not necessary for humanity to know.

It depends on who you're talking to through that person. Some spirits of light have humor, and some don't want to make it easy for you... When they explain a difficult matter, sometimes it sounds for you like it's conflicting. But if you ask more questions about it you will understand, and it actually makes sense. So if you ask more questions and do more research, you will in the end find out what you will feel is the right thing, and your understanding will be greater... But you only get exactly what you ask. You don't get any extra.

Andy also directly asked Naomi's elders to talk a little about themselves:

We are highly evolved souls and we are chosen – elected – to do this work... We come from all spheres... We have had different training and come up through different paths, and even though we are advanced souls

138

we still have different strengths... We tune into the one Source, which is all pervasive and prevalent. But different souls have access to different levels of information from the Source.

A useful analogy here might be to the group of blind people asked to describe an elephant by feel alone, with each of them coming up with a different report dependant upon the part of its anatomy they were touching. So, at least as far as the more complex questions are concerned, this research is not an infallible, black-and-white process. And hopefully the presentation and analysis of answers reflects this fact, while still giving a strong lead as to any favored interpretation of the evidence.

Subject Feedback

After the research sessions had been completed we wrote to all our subjects and – in addition to the *specific* feedback on potential prior knowledge of and conscious interference in particular topics, as discussed in the Introduction – we asked for their *general* feedback on the experience. This was most revealing, because not only did nearly all of them seem to feel that they had not consciously interfered with the process to any significant degree, but a number of other common themes emerged.

David was typical in that he had little doubt that for the bulk of the time it was his sources coming through:

> On reading the transcript I notice that I was speaking both in the first and third person, and I remember that for much of the session I felt like an interested spectator rather than a participant. In fact, when I read some of the more insightful comments in it I had an 'I wish I'd said that' moment!

He also made the following additional observation: 'I remember feeling at times that there was much more information to be had, and that it was important to ask the right questions.' This echoes Katrine's comment in the last section that 'you only get what you ask for', and it seems to suggest that further work on refining the questions for any future research might pay handsome dividends.

Meanwhile, although I have already indicated that our subjects always spoke in their own voices, several of them tended to focus on the extent to which their transcripts revealed a *mode* of speech that was unfamiliar to them. Here are Veronica, Nadine and Denise:

> I have never gone as deeply into the interlife realms as on this occasion. I was able to remember vivid details of the experience I had before.

However, this time I can only remember about five minutes' worth of the experience, and I'm sure I was in a deep trance during the session and that my conscious mind – although in the background – was not able to come forward. On looking over the transcript I don't recognize either the questions or my tone of phrase in answering.

All of the transcript makes sense to me and I agree with what was said. However I felt the tone and my choice of words were somewhat different to how I would normally say things – it felt as though they represented an innate knowledge that came from within, and that at times I was 'conferring' in order to say things in a precise or understandable way. The Atlantis question was unusual because I have heard about Atlantis, of course, but I was surprised to read that I said 'that name is not recognizable to me' – I can only assume it is an earth-given name that has no relevance to the spirit world.

Initially in the sessions I think I was concerned that nothing would happen but, as soon as I felt the tremendous energy surround me physically and became aware that my breathing was changing, I knew it was not me. Although I think the conscious mind tends to float in and out and it is possible to question and doubt yourself, as the information starts to come through then it is easy to flow and relax with the whole experience. Afterwards I only recalled snatches of the information. But, looking at the transcript, many of the questions dealt with issues I had not previously considered and had no knowledge of. And the answers are not ones that I would have been able to give you in full waking consciousness. I would have been much more vague, I would have stumbled, hesitated and had to think about them. And I would have found it difficult to comprehend exactly what you meant by some of the questions. But at that time I had no difficulty in answering them, and I felt no doubt that what I was saying was absolutely correct – although sometimes it was hard to actually speak and communicate, because so much more was going on for me, and it was as if every cell in and around my body was receiving messages that my mouth had to relay. So I feel it was pure information from another source. And as I read the words I could again see some of the images I was shown at the time. It was this feeling that let me know that the information given was special, even though before reading the transcript I was probably more cynical of it than others would be. So it has been a great personal reminder for me – I guess to remember truths that my own personal ego has tried to discount or disbelieve.

By contrast Alva, Claire and Amy all tended to emphasize the extent to which they were surprised by, or even uncomfortable with, some of their answers:

I have never been in a deeper trance and the replies came from my subconscious mind. For example, when you asked me about how long ago humans came to earth, I answered and at the same time wondered how this could be right.

I cannot tell to what extent my conscious mind interfered with the session. I was certainly in deep trance, but I was aware of my conscious mind being active occasionally. Having said that, sometimes this manifested as answers coming through that surprised me – I can remember thinking, 'wow, I didn't know that!' a couple of times.

Although I was 'mentally' present I sometimes seemed to have no control over what they said, even to the extent of being aware of not liking the answer I was giving, even though it's what they said. And at other times I felt like a go-between. It was also difficult to differentiate between what I knew and what I didn't. It's as though being 'joined' mentally with them meant that I knew what they knew but sometimes it was really difficult to explain it in human terms. Then there were the questions that the elders threw back at you [in section 4.2], because they wanted *you* to give the answer. 'I' wasn't asking that. Each time they asked you 'what would be the point in that?' they wanted you to think about it.

Naomi too picked up on the difficulty of expressing some of the 'pure' information in understandable, human terms:

The answers generally came to me as a 'knowing', and sometimes they came as an image – although I do remember feeling frustrated a couple of times at not being able to find adequate words to get my answer across, even though I understood the concept. But at others the words would be there automatically with no effort required on my part.

Meanwhile Claire and Nora confirmed Naomi's feeling that sometimes their answers flowed much more than others:

The nature of the experience was mixed. Earlier in the session it was more telepathic, but sometimes later on there seemed to be more interference from my conscious mind. But most of the information surprised me.

As always, I've been wondering about how much I 'made up' myself, although it didn't feel like that. But it wasn't the same all the way through. With some questions, the answers just came so easily, even though they were things I don't think I've really thought about before. With other questions I felt I was interfering more, especially with questions that had an 'earthly' answer – like when the human race first emerged, and Atlantis. On the more 'soul' questions, it was different.

Amy also added that she felt that different elders helped her with different areas, which further confirmed our prior suspicion that not all of our sources had the same knowledge or expertise:

> My experience of the research session was different to other sessions. It felt like a normal regression until we moved onto the research questions. Then I became aware of a separation between my body and my soul energy. Each time you asked a set of questions the energy changed. I was aware of how, each time it shifted, it felt like a different vibration. I was told that as you changed the subject matter the elder who was most experienced in that subject gave the answers, because each one has their own speciality.

There is one other aspect of our research that I have not yet mentioned. One of our sources specifically suggested that Andy himself should act as a research subject, more than anything so he could experience what it was like to be on the other side of the process, and then report back on it. So when all the other sessions had been completed, our colleague and friend Duncan Bain Smith kindly agreed to regress Andy and ask the same set of questions. This time I sat in on the session as well, partly to prompt Duncan with various notes, and partly to gain some first-hand exposure to the process for myself.

Rather like Veronica and Denise's descriptions of their surroundings in the Introduction, Andy found that he was not with any elders or other beings of light, but merely in the appropriate 'energy space' to attempt to answer the questions. Moreover he agreed with some of the subjects in that he felt at times his answers flowed almost before the question had been asked, while at others they were less forthcoming – at which point there was sufficient time for his conscious mind to start to interfere. Indeed this much seemed reasonably obvious just from observing the session.

Despite this, the information he provided was in almost every respect consistent with the majority opinion that had already formed in the previous sessions. Of course, although he had not read through any of the transcripts of the other sessions at the time, at the very least his subconscious memory would have been aware of the majority of the answers that had previously been given. So we cannot use his own responses as any sort of definitive confirmation. Nevertheless his most important feedback was his feeling that, even when he was sometimes aware that he was repeating information from previous sessions, he was equally aware that only the information that really resonated with him was coming to the surface. It may therefore be reasonable to suggest that, even when a subject did have prior knowledge about any given area, often it would equally be only those aspects that really resonated at a deeply intuitive level that came to the fore. Having said that, we have also seen that our subjects were often amazed by the new information or different viewpoints they – or their sources – produced.

Summary

There can be little doubt that some of our research information came from our subjects' conscious interference and prior knowledge, despite all our attempted safeguards – including Andy's expertise in keeping them in an appropriate depth of trance during the sessions, and my attempts to screen out obviously dubious material by a combination of investigating prior knowledge and using my intuition.

Nevertheless, they themselves maintain that the bulk of the information they provided did not come from them but from their ethereal sources, and two major factors seem to bear this out. On the one hand, especially with the first group of questions but also in some other areas, they consistently provided a unanimous view about issues that, while commonly known and discussed, often cause heated debate. On the other, they also provided certain profound insights about issues that are rarely even raised – for example, about how experience is continuously recycled back to the Source in section 2.3, and how repetitive behavior is not necessarily aberrant in section 2.4.

As to the broader and more universally pertinent messages that emerge from this research, I would suggest there are three that really stand out:

- *The Holographic Soul*: The most effective way to bring together the strong evidence that soul consciousness is part of a unified whole with the equally strong evidence that it can also be individual is to propose that it is holographic. That is to say, we are both individual aspects of the Source, and full holographic representations of it, all at the same time. However this does not mean that soul individuality is in itself an illusion. The definition of a hologram is that the part contains the whole, and yet at the same time is clearly distinguishable from it.

- *Learning, Experience and Growth*: The most effective way to explain the strong evidence that souls not only make progressive choices, but also engage in repetitive patterns of behavior especially when they are less experienced, is to recognize that the aim of all reincarnating souls is to learn, experience and grow. This is entirely consistent with the Source's primary aim, which is to experience all that is and can be. So as individualized aspects of the Source who have chosen to reincarnate on this planet, we are merely fulfilling a small part of that objective by gaining a balance of all the experiences available via this route.

- *Planning, Responsibility and Free Will*: Interlife regression evidence consistently indicates that most of us actively choose and plan our lives before we return. This means that when we face difficult circumstances we would do well to accept personal responsibility, because not only did we choose them, but we did so to learn from them. And we will not achieve this by ignoring them, or by attempting to blame other people, a capricious deity or blind chance. Moreover, any previews we have during the interlife merely represent major probabilities and lesser possibilities. We still have complete free will to stray from our most probable, chosen life path, because a totally predetermined experience would provide no opportunity for growth.

Final Messages

5.3 Are there any final messages or anything else you think it is important for us to know at this time?

These final messages from David, Alva, Denise, Amy, Naomi, Nadine and Claire incorporate a gradual build-up of advice concerning understanding, intuition, reconnection, responsibility, potential, trust and – ultimately – living in love with a full awareness that we are all part of the One:

Know yourself... When you know your true nature, then greed and anger and fear will be put in their right places, and you will be able to live in a way that is right for you and for the planet as well... The key for the healthy future of humanity lies in understanding, at a personal and global level. Only by understanding our true nature can we grow... We need to be able to see humanity for what it is a force that has the potential for great destruction both of the environment and of itself, but also the potential to be divine... If we can it will be the difference between being blind and seeing; between being deaf and hearing; between being a prisoner and being free.

We must go into ourselves. The single most important thing each and every one of us has to do is to find the internal balance point... If you are in balance, this will glow, and be radiant, and affect everyone that comes into your field. And that will be the greatest learning of all... Like a stone dropped in water, it will just make bigger and bigger ripples. And each and every soul will find their own way to move it forward, to give it to other people around. Some will write books, some will sing, some will paint, some will use other forms of communication and creativity. If you learn to feel with your intuition, and then act, you will always do the right thing. It might not be perfect, but it will be right.

We need to stimulate interest in the possibilities for the human race. In the ability they all have to start to use the powers available to them to work with conscious thought and the power of the subconscious mind. And to see their true potential to create heaven on earth... Traditional religions haven't helped, even though that was their original intention... They have been selective and exclusive, and humans have made one right to make another wrong. The individual needs to be reminded, not the group. Personal reconnection is required for every soul... This requires smaller groups not affiliated to any religion to provide comfort and connection and support; to nurture individuals; to remind them of the truth, and of how to make faith non-exclusive and part of everyday life; and to help them to remember they hold the seed within, and to look within themselves. Humans are too quick to look to others to solve problems and issues.

Historically we have been too busy looking for a savior, instead of saving ourselves and being responsible... It's an evolutionary thing, it will depend on how quickly humanity accepts new beliefs. Sometimes it can take upwards of two or three hundred years to fully bring in a new belief system. Look historically at how long it took to bring Christianity into full play, and other systems. Right now, we're only on the edge... But always keep searching for the truth, never settle. Truth is many-layered, and one truth will lead on to another.

There need to be stronger communities, teaching communities for the spirit, and a shift away from materialism and the importance of strict scientific discovery... More people need to follow their intuition and their heart, and to let go of material desires... Everything is overcome by love, and by a peaceful and community approach. That can only be done gradually, and now people are becoming more aware. And communities with spiritual awareness need to come together more, and have a louder voice... Above all, take each step of every day on the basis of unconditional love, looking to your inner self to take the sensible and loving course.

The most important thing that needs to be done is to trigger off the resonance of excitement about a new plane of awareness... The excitement of something new, something better, that will stimulate an opening of awareness of potentials of who and what you are, and what you can become... And trust. Become more. Know who you are... Through trust comes acceptance, and through acceptance comes compassion, and through compassion comes the ultimate feeling of love for your Oneness.

It's important for those who are waking up to lead by example... By living in love because you are aware that everyone is One, and loving yourself because of what you are... By opening people's awareness to possibilities, so that each can come to realize what he or she truly is... And just remember that you are loved more than you can possibly know, and that each and every one of you is part of the Source, part of the One.

It would be presumptuous to even attempt to add to these inspiring messages of hope, compassion and love.

Postscript

I cannot finally close without mentioning certain further messages that came through from Denise, Alva, Nora, David and Veronica. These seem to relate primarily to the dissemination of this type of research, which attempts to ground spirituality in a more rational and logical framework than it has hitherto enjoyed:

> This is a time of great possibility. It's a good time for a new message, for new awakenings to allow modern humans to accept and understand.

> This is an important piece of work to raise human energy levels and awareness... I am getting a strong feeling of light and love here.

> It is a good thing to reach many people like this... The different parts of the book will reach out to the different people that read it, each one will take from it what they need. And talking about it will reach different people... My council says the world needs this work, so it is a pleasure to help.

> The spreading of knowledge about the true nature of humanity is vital, it's one of the most important things that's happening right now... Statistics and rational analysis will make it feel more real, because people who do not believe at the moment will be more likely to believe in that.

> There are those who find it hard to just accept, and they need to be presented with scientific and logical proof in order to believe. That is where any research of this kind is incredibly helpful. It also allows people to validate things they believe within but feel unable to express to others.

So if you find that the messages in this book resonate deeply with you, you might feel moved to spread the word – not only about this research but also about the underlying message of 'Rational Spirituality' developed in *The Book of the Soul* and on my website.

APPENDIX I
RESEARCH APPROACH AND PROTOCOLS

The Mechanics of Interlife Regression

Andy covers the techniques used in interlife regression in detail in his first book *Healing the Eternal Soul*. But, to summarize, the altered state of consciousness or trance induced by hypnosis focuses the mind inwards. Approximately 15 percent of the population are highly receptive and move quickly into trance; some 70 percent are moderately receptive, so that a longer induction or repeated sessions are required; and the remaining 15 percent are either non-responsive, or will only respond minimally. In addition, it seems that people enter the trance state more quickly and deeply when they have previously experienced such altered states.

For a *past-life* regression a subject only needs to be in the alpha state of altered awareness. This is achieved through a light hypnosis induction, which will normally take some 10 to 15 minutes, although meditation or other techniques for inward focusing on past-life memories can also be used. But for an *interlife* regression subjects need to be in the theta state, which is the deepest level before entering sleep. At these deeper levels the subject's conscious mind is inactive and they are able to intuitively link to the details of their soul memories. This state is best achieved by up to 45 minutes of trance induction and gradual deepening. But there is no significant tendency for people to be able to enter the alpha but *not* the theta state – so anyone who responds to hypnosis should be able to regress not only to a past life but also to the interlife.

Of course the therapist needs to be able to assess the depth of trance and, although this is not an exact science, there are physical pointers. As the subject goes deeper their blood circulation slows, their face becomes paler, their breathing becomes shallower, all body movements cease, their bottom lip starts to droop, and there is an onset of regular and involuntary swallowing. Most interlife therapists find that the easiest way to check on initial trance depth is to ask the subject to respond by raising a finger.

148

Deeper trance states increase the delay in response, the finger adopts a slow, jerky movement, and the command is interpreted literally so that the finger stays aloft until it is acknowledged. Moreover, when a subject talks there will be a similarly increased delay in, and literal response to, questions, and their voice will become quieter.

Having said that, as soon as subjects start to talk about their experience, some trance depth is lost. The main techniques for maintaining it are to trigger an 'anchor' that has previously been created at a deep point, or to have periods of silence so the subject can focus on the inner experience. But once the intuitive link is established it tends to remain in place, even if lighter levels of trance occur. The key is to spot if a subject has lost the intuitive link and drifted to a conscious level, and this is achieved by checking for literal responses and assessing the quality of the voice. Indeed in some cases a subject will interrupt the session themselves to say that their conscious mind has become active. But provided trance depth has previously been created and the intuitive link has been established, most interlife regression sessions can continue in excess of two hours without problems.

The Subjects

	Age	*Sex*	*Country*
Nadine	30s	F	UK
David	40s	M	UK
Veronica	30s	F	UK
Alva	40s	F	Norway
Katrine	30s	F	Norway
Nora	20s	F	Norway
Amy	40s	F	UK
Denise	30s	F	UK
Claire	40s	F	UK
Naomi	30s	F	UK

Andy selected ten initial subjects who he felt would be good candidates, in most cases because he had conducted at least one personal interlife session with them before. Although only one was male, this should not be taken to mean that men are less suited to this type of work – it merely reflects the fact that he tends to have more female than male clients. However, for reasons that will be explained shortly, we were sufficiently concerned about three of the original subjects' sessions that we felt we could not use them. As a result Andy had to conduct three additional sessions with new subjects.

The profile of the final ten, in terms of age, sex and country of residence, is shown above in session date order.

The Questions

The subject matter of the questions had two major influences. One objective was to focus on those areas of existing regression and other spiritual research that have remained contentious because different commentators continue to express different views about them. The other more general influence was to examine a variety of broader historical and philosophical topics that have consistently intrigued deep thinkers of all persuasions.

Of course it would be ridiculous to pretend that subjective bias, and the broad spiritual framework we adhere to, did not play a part in the formulation of the questions. For example, given that we were using the interlife experience to induce the sessions, it would have been nonsensical for us to ask the question 'do individual souls reincarnate?' – because this is, in itself, a fundamental inference of interlife research. On the other hand it was perfectly reasonable for us to ask '*why* do we reincarnate?' On top of this, my previous research in both *Genesis Unveiled* and *The Book of the Soul* played a significant part. So everyone will doubtless experience some frustration about their particular pet topics that we might have included, but clearly we had to prioritize to keep our research manageable. Nevertheless we attempted to cover a broad spectrum of major spiritual, historical and philosophical questions that are of universal interest.

We also made every attempt to keep our primary questions as open as possible, in the hope that at this level at least Andy would not be unduly leading the subjects. So, to take the first question as an example, despite the strong evidence that some souls remain at least temporarily trapped and fail to move into the light straight after physical death, we asked the open question '*can* a soul become trapped etc.?' instead of making prior assumptions. The secondary or follow-up questions were then designed to explore the various possibilities contingent on the first answer and, although these sometimes contained quite specific information from that first answer, Andy still attempted to minimize any deliberate leading. We also expected that subjects would require different levels of prompting, with some providing 'chapter and verse' on the given topic from the primary question alone, while others might be more reticent and require further prompting via the secondary questions. And this is indeed how it proved, as we have seen.

On the subject of potential leading, we should also consider whether it would have been possible for Andy's own worldview and expectations to subconsciously, or psychically, influence our subjects. We cannot completely discount this possibility, especially when *intent* can have an incredibly strong psychic impact as we have seen. However, there are a number of factors that appear to reduce the likelihood of this having significantly affected the quality of our research. First, Andy himself did not necessarily have a great deal of prior knowledge of some of the topics, especially in the third and fourth groups of questions. Second, our subjects quite often contradicted him when he asked specific follow-up questions, especially when he was exploring certain areas more deeply. Third, on occasion they came up with information that neither of us had considered before. All of this suggests that subconscious or psychic leading by Andy did not play a major role.

The Sessions

Whenever an interlife regression takes place, the subject must first be taken back to a past life and then led into the interlife that follows it. Depending on the ease with which they entered and adapted to that state, Andy would conduct a longer or shorter personal interlife session before turning to the universal questions.

Most sessions lasted between three and four hours in total, with between two and three hours devoted to our research. Indeed Andy soon found that they were unusually draining on the subjects, and he would engage in a short period of healing immediately after each session to settle their energy fields. He also found it was sensible at the beginning of each session to anchor the idea that, if they had exhausted their capacity to pass on useful information after a certain period of time, he should be given a sign – such as the deliberate blocking of information, or some sort of physical discomfort in the subject. This meant that in several cases more than one session had to be conducted, with one subject, Denise, providing over six hours of research material over the course of three sessions.

The sessions were also draining for Andy himself. The combination of the concentration required for such complex and pioneering work, and the high-level spiritual energies that the subjects were tapping into, both took their toll, which is why he had to space the sessions out. But his perseverance and endurance, as well as that of our subjects, were well rewarded.

As for the order of the questions, for the first three sessions with Nadine, David and Veronica, question groups 1 to 4 were taken in order. Then in the next five sessions with Alva, Katrine, Nora, Amy and Denise we reversed the order, taking group 4 first and group 1 last. Finally in the last two sessions with Claire and Naomi we took the groups in the order 2, 3, 4, 1. We did this because both Andy and our subjects tended to be fresher at the beginning of a session than at the end, so we were attempting to give each group a fair chance – albeit recognizing that the questions tended to get progressively harder in their standard order. This does mean that Andy spent different amounts of time on different groups with each subject, usually giving more to those that came first, and as a general rule our subjects' answers were correspondingly variable in length and detail.

The sessions were conducted between January and September 2006.

Processing the Information

The following are the details of the criteria I applied when evaluating the research material we obtained.

1 Is the answer relevant to our research?

Especially in the earlier sessions when Andy was getting to grips with the exact meaning of some of the questions, they were not always phrased as clearly as they could have been. This meant that in some instances literal answers were given to the question asked, but it was not what we were really interested in. In addition to this, sometimes a session would go off on something of a tangent. Usually this information has been omitted unless it happens to be relevant to another topic, or is particularly revealing in its own right.

2 Does the answer make enough sense to be used?

English is not the first language of our three Norwegian subjects, which merely added to the difficulties they faced in attempting to describe sometimes difficult concepts. In addition all our subjects' answers tended to vary in their general lucidity over the course of a whole session. And on a few occasions, especially with the more complex questions, some responses were so convoluted or incoherent that it was impossible to establish what the subject was really trying to say – unless Andy happened to press them to explain, which would work sometimes but not always. This is not a criticism, because as we have seen they were sometimes struggling to put difficult non-human concepts into a language we could understand. But it does mean that some material of this nature had to be omitted.

3 How likely is it that any prior knowledge has influenced the information?

Our list of questions was sufficiently broad and general that it would have been almost impossible to find subjects who had absolutely no prior knowledge of any of the topics covered. However we did apply a number of controls. First, in order to try to eliminate the possibility of their conscious minds 'second-guessing' the answers, we did not show them the questions in advance. Second, we subsequently gave them transcripts of their sessions and asked them to identify any sections that surprised them – either because they contradicted previously held views, or because they had no prior knowledge of the information they gave. Third, we subsequently asked them whether they had read particular sources of information that I regarded as being of relevance to particular answers, which therefore might have influenced them. All of this feedback has been incorporated into the analysis in the main chapters where appropriate.

This latter was in addition to ascertaining the following information about more general potential influences. Virtually all of our subjects had some degree of previous exposure to Michael Newton's interlife research. Only Veronica had *not* read his first book, *Journey of Souls*, although only half of them – Amy, Alva, Katrine, Naomi and David – had read his second and more detailed book, *Destiny of Souls*. However his research is only relevant to some of the questions, and these are primarily in the first two groups. By contrast, very few of them had read *The Book of the Soul* before their research sessions. Most had never seen it and, although Claire, Denise and Nora had briefly flicked through especially the early parts, only David had read it properly. Moreover none of them had read *Genesis Unveiled*. This is important because, as already indicated, these two were far more ubiquitous sources for all four groups of questions.

Nor had I met or corresponded with any of our subjects before the research sessions, apart from a brief meeting with David.

It is also worth noting that when, for example, a subject has read a particular book a long time ago, they might not *consciously* remember all its contents, but a significant proportion will almost certainly be logged somewhere in their *subconscious* mind. And clearly it would not be impossible for such details to emerge under regression. So any discussion of conscious interference must sensibly include potential subconscious interference as well.

4 Does the subject's ego seem to be consciously interfering?

If we now turn to the extent to which personal ego might have interfered in the research process, the three original sessions that we deemed unreliable were replaced primarily for this reason. In all three the subject responded using 'I' and talked very much from their own human and sometimes ego-driven perspective.

By contrast, in our finally selected sessions the subjects consistently although not exclusively talked from the perspective of the elders or other beings of light with whom they had linked, rather than from a human or earth perspective. So they often responded using 'we', and referred to 'humans' or 'you', and to 'there' for earth and 'here' for the light realms. All of this suggested they were acting as a relatively objective channel for the information. Indeed, Katrine specifically confirmed our supposition about the perspective used:

> Some souls have more ability to be channels and have access to higher spirits of light who then talk directly to you, whereas when that does not happen it's easier for the soul to interfere.

Was the question asked?

There is one other factor that came into play in the answers presented here, and that is whether any given question was actually put to a particular subject. Andy found that it was important to let the session flow and, by not sticking rigidly to the format of the secondary questions, let the information coming from the subject guide him. Coupled with our fine-tuning of the questions especially during the first few sessions, this does mean that not all subjects were directly asked all secondary questions – although sometimes they volunteered the appropriate information themselves. In addition, occasionally even a primary question was missed with a subject, purely as an oversight, although sometimes Andy then asked a relevant secondary question that effectively answered the primary question as well.

Summary

To sum up, the decisions about the research information to present in this book were made as follows. Three sessions were discarded completely, primarily because of significant, conscious, ego interference. Then, with the remaining ten sessions, the following procedures were used:

- If a question was never asked, of course the answer could not be included.

- If an answer, or part thereof, was not relevant or simply made no sense, it has been excluded.

- If a subject's conscious knowledge was obviously interfering in an answer then it has been either fully or partially excluded. This would tend to be because it exhibited a *combination* of other factors. These include, for example, being significantly at odds with any majority opinion; making only partial sense; contradicting something they had said elsewhere; or if they admitted in their feedback that they had significant prior knowledge of the topic that figured heavily in their answer.

- By contrast, if an answer was markedly different from majority opinion but there was no other reason to regard it as suspect, it has *not* been excluded.

The result is that all relevant and sensible answers to both primary and secondary questions where conscious interference was not strongly suspected have been presented here, even if only the key points have been taken rather than presenting them in full. For completeness if any subject was not asked *any* of the questions in a primary section this has been noted, but this only happened on seven occasions. But every subject who was asked at least *some* of the questions in a primary section went on to provide some sort of relevant response. This means that, at a primary level, 203 answers have been included either in full or in part. This represents 97 percent of the potential maximum of 210 – or 21 primary topics across 10 sessions. Generally speaking this extent of inclusion of answers is testament to their quality and to the process being used.

As to the potential accusations of selectivity that might still be made, in general it should be clear that answers have been included even when they contradicted any majority view – provided they were coherent or at least interesting, and there was no obvious reason to suspect conscious interference in that particular area. Moreover they have also regularly been included even when they contradicted my own previously held views. I trust this will go some way towards deflecting potential criticism of this nature.

APPENDIX II

THE RESEARCH QUESTIONS

1. Unusual Soul Behavior

1.1. **After physical death can soul energy fail to move into the light and become trapped in earth's astral plane?**

    1.1.1. If so, why does this occur?

    1.1.2. Is it the entire soul energy that was originally brought down that becomes trapped, or merely a fragment?

    1.1.3. Will these energies always move into the light and be reunited in the end?

    1.1.4. Is there a difference between a fragment and an imprint?

    1.1.5. How often does this occur?

1.2. **Can soul energy trapped on earth attach itself to other people?**

    1.2.1. If so, why does this occur?

    1.2.2. What are the effects on the host?

    1.2.3. Can this ever be planned?

    1.2.4. How often does this occur?

    1.2.5. What happens to the attachment when the host dies?

1.3. **Can we lose soul fragments while still incarnate?**

    1.3.1. If so, why does this occur?

    1.3.2. Must these fragments rejoin the rest of the soul at some point?

    1.3.3. What can we do to avoid losing or attracting soul fragments?

1.4. **Can a soul have two or more incarnations at the same time?**

    1.4.1. If so, why does this occur, and are there any risks?

    1.4.2. How often does this occur?

1.5. **Can a soul vacate its adult body so another soul can walk in?**

    1.5.1. If not, why not?

1.6. **Can a soul experience the complete past life of another soul?**

1.6.1.   If so, why does this occur?

1.6.2.   Is there any essential difference between a shared soul memory and a genuine life of our own in the physical plane?

1.6.3.   Would a regression subject be able to tell the difference between their own and other people's past lives?

1.6.4.   Can past-life regression sessions include 'projections' to help our learning or healing?

1.7.   Can physical characteristics be carried from one life to another?

1.7.1.   Can traumatic body memories be carried over?

1.7.2.   Can facial features be carried over?

1.7.3.   How does this process work?

1.8.   To what extent is the death-point preplanned?

1.8.1.   How are suicides viewed in the light realms?

1.8.2.   Are suicides ever preplanned?

1.9.   Are there any real demonic beings?

1.9.1.   If not, are there any non-human 'dark forces' acting outside of the 'plan'?

2.   Soul Development

2.1.   What is the purpose of reincarnating on the physical plane?

2.1.1.   Can some souls choose not to reincarnate?

2.1.2.   Can you comment on the suggestion that the reincarnation cycle is just an illusion, and that when this is recognized a soul can return to the Source?

2.1.3.   Why does the Source manifest into all the forms in the universe in the first place?

2.2.   Are there differences between human and animal soul energy?

2.2.1.   Can human souls develop from animal souls?

2.3.   How are new souls created?

2.3.1.   At some point will the Source draw all soul energy back into itself, and then start the whole process of creation again in an endless cycle?

2.4.   Do all souls have a full interlife experience every time?

2.4.1. Why do some souls seem to display repetitive behavior over many lifetimes?

2.4.2. Why do some people appear to have a blank interlife experience under regression?

2.4.3. Can interlife regression experiences be projections to help us rather than genuine memories?

2.5. What happens to souls once they no longer need to reincarnate?

2.5.1. What roles can more experienced souls take?

2.6. Can souls from earth gain experience on other planets?

2.6.1. What is the nature of life on other planets? Are any of them comparable to the earth experience?

3. Humanity's Past and Future

3.1. When did the modern human race first emerge?

3.1.1. Were there experiments to bring advanced soul energy into the earth plane before the human form evolved?

3.2. Are any of the myths of lost continents and civilizations true?

3.3. How is the exponential human population increase on earth being satisfied from a soul perspective?

3.3.1. Are new human souls still being created?

3.3.2. Are souls coming back with greater frequency?

3.3.3. Are more souls from other planets or dimensions incarnating on earth?

3.4. What is the biggest problem facing humanity at the moment?

3.4.1. How is global warming viewed, and what needs to be done?

3.4.2. Do we need a major global catastrophe to initiate a fresh start?

3.4.3. Are our global political systems seriously jeopardizing our spiritual development?

3.4.4. Are there any major plans to assist humanity's spiritual development? If so, do they involve more evolved souls incarnating, or a lifting of the veil of amnesia?

4. Reality and Time

4.1. Do we create our own reality by the power of our thoughts and intentions?

    4.1.1. Why do we not always achieve the outcomes we desire?

    4.1.2. Can interaction with other people's life plans or intentions restrict this ability?

4.2. Can you explain how the notion of time really works?

    4.2.1. Are there multiple, physical, earth realities all playing out in parallel?

    4.2.2. Can we go back in time and alter events?

    4.2.3. Are our individual futures already known?

    4.2.4. Is our collective future already known?

5. Concluding Questions

5.1. How can we tell if the subject's conscious knowledge is interfering with this research process?

5.2. What are the possible reasons for us obtaining conflicting answers from different subjects?

5.3. Are there any final messages or anything else you think it is important for us to know at this time?

GLOSSARY

Note that words or phrases in italics can be traced to their own glossary entry.

Altruistic Life: A new phrase coined to reflect lives that are deliberately planned and chosen to be of service to others, which tends to be a characteristic of *progressive behavior*. Because such lives do not involve learning for the soul themselves but for those around them, that soul's free will to divert from the planned *life path* can be reduced.

Altruistic Skills: A new phrase coined to reflect the particular skills, such as teaching, guiding, healing, energy work and so on, that souls increasingly train in as they become more experienced and engage in more *progressive behavior*. A *soul group* can come together to work on particular skills, just as it can to work on *emotional lessons*.

Astral Realms/Plane: The realm, closely linked to the physical or earth plane, in which *trapped spirits* and *elementals* reside, possibly in different aspects.

Attachments: *Trapped soul energies* or *fragments* that after death have attached themselves to an incarnate person, place or object rather than returning to the *light realms*.

Body Traumas: Emotional traumas from past lives that are so intense they are psychically imprinted on the new energy and hence physical body. They can be carried over unintentionally, in which case they are *unresolved emotions* that form part of a *reactive pattern*, with the body trauma acting as a reminder or *trigger*. Or they can be carried over by choice as part of a *proactive pattern*, in which case they are in-progress emotions with which the soul wants to carry on working.

Conscious Co-Creation: Deliberate attempts by incarnate people to band together with united mental and spiritual focus, in the hope of affecting some aspect of events or activities on the earth plane.

Core Soul Energy: That holographic portion of energy that is left behind in the *light realms* when a soul reincarnates. This energy will be more active or dormant depending on what proportion of the total it represents.

Delayering: A new phrase coined to describe the automatic process of healing and energy lightening that all souls must receive in order to make the transition to the *light realms* proper.

Elder Level: The level in the *light realms* in which the *elders* reside, which is at a higher energy vibration than the *Guide/Group Level*.

Elders: The wise and experienced souls who assist those still incarnating with *past-life review* and *next-life planning* advice and guidance at a higher level than that of *spirit guides*.

Elementals: Nature spirits and other soul energies that are closely connected to particular animal, vegetable or mineral forms on the earth plane, and that reside in their own aspect of the *astral plane*.

Emotional Lessons: The standard emotions that all souls attempt to master while in the physical plane by experiencing both sides of each. Members of the same *soul group* will often be working on the same lesson together.

Fragments: Portions of soul energy that can split off after death even though the bulk of the soul energy returns to the *light plane*. These can remain trapped in the *astral plane*, or form *attachments* to other incarnate people, places or objects. They will however be reunited with their *core soul energy* at some point.

Grey Place: An aspect of the *Transition Level* in which *trapped soul energies* can remain because of *unresolved emotions* that they are not yet prepared to have properly healed. This is one step up from remaining trapped in the *astral plane*.

Guide/Group Level: The level in the *light realms* in which reincarnating *soul groups* and their *spirit guides* reside, which is at a lower energy vibration than the *Elder Level*. There are different *vibration aspects* of this level.

Higher Levels: The levels in the *light realms* that are at a higher vibration than those of the *elders*, about which we can say little other than that they would progressively approach the *Source* itself.

Holographic Soul: A new phrase coined to reflect the fact that soul consciousness is holographic. That is, we are both individual aspects of the *Source*, and full holographic representations of it, all at the same time.

Imprints: Soul energies that remain in the *astral plane* after death and may be differentiable from *fragments*. If so this will be both because they are more passive, and because they do not need to be reunited with their *core soul energy*.

Interlife: The experience of being between incarnate lives in the *light realms*, also known as the life between lives.

Life Path: The most probable course of any given incarnate life if that person makes the decisions that they have planned in the *light realms*. The soul may also have agreed certain *triggers* that are intended to prompt them to stay on that path.

Life Previews: The foretaste of the next life received in the *light realms*, which represents the major probabilities and lesser possibilities for that life. These can be multiple or single previews.

Light Realms/Plane: The true home of all soul energies, and the plane most closely connected with the *Source* itself.

Multiple Incarnations: The holographic splitting of soul energy so that it can experience two or more incarnations concurrently.

Next-Life Planning: The whole process that encompasses life previews, and planning discussions with *elders*, *spirit guides* and *soul mates*.

Parallel Dimensions/Worlds: The idea that there may be multiple earth realities playing out in parallel.

Past-Life Review: The process of contemplating and learning from the last incarnate life, which will usually involve an element of discussion with *elders*, *spirit guides* and *soul mates*.

Proactive Patterns: A new phrase coined to describe patterns of *repetitive behavior* in which the soul chooses to carry the same in-progress emotions into a new life, in order to carry on working with them in the physical plane and to complete the appropriate *emotional lesson*.

Progressive Behavior: Behavior increasingly engaged in by souls as they gain in experience, typified by leading *altruistic lives* and developing *altruistic skills*.

Projections: Experiences of past lives or interlives under *regression* that may not be genuine, but rather are projected by *spirit guides* or other helpers to assist the recipient's learning or healing.

Quantum Theory: The scientific theory that at the sub-atomic level quantum energy packets have the properties of probability waves until such point as they are observed, at which point either the wave function collapses into only one observed physical reality, or multiple *parallel worlds* are created to reflect each possibility.

Reactive Patterns: A new phrase coined to describe patterns of *repetitive behavior* in which the soul carries over strong *unresolved emotions* unintentionally, usually as a result of incomplete healing, review and planning in the *light realms*.

Regression: The process by which subjects are placed in an altered state of consciousness so that they can recall elements of past lives or the *interlife*. This is usually achieved by hypnosis, but other methods can be used.

Relayering: A new phrase coined to describe the process of taking on the emotions and strengths that a soul wants to work on, or with, in the next incarnate life.

Repetitive Behavior: Behavior that tends to be engaged in by less experienced souls, typified either by *reactive* or *proactive patterns*.

Shared Soul Memories: The process by which souls can share their past-life experiences in the *light realms* to assist the learning process.

Soul Energy Reintegration: The process by which returning soul energy is reunited with the *core soul energy* left behind in the *light realms*.

Soul Fragmentation: The process by which, in intense emotional interactions, incarnate souls can lose fragments of their energy to others. These will be automatically reunited with the host after death, as part of the *delayering* process.

Soul Groups: Groups of *soul mates* who work closely together both in the *light realms* and in successions of lives in the physical plane.

Soul Mates: The other members of a *soul group* who work closely together both in the *light realms* and in successions of lives in the physical plane.

Source: The Ultimate Source of everything in the universe itself, and of which all individual soul consciousnesses are *holographic soul* aspects.

Spirit Guides: Specialist souls who spend a long time training to help others with the opportunities offered and problems encountered in both the light and physical planes. They provide guidance and advice during *past-life review* and *next-life planning* at a lower level to that of the *elders*. Especially less experienced guides may well still be reincarnating on the physical plane.

Spirit Realms: Another term for the *light realms* often used by regression subjects, although we tend to avoid it because of potential confusion with the *astral plane* in which *trapped spirits* reside.

Spirits of Light: Another term often used for *elders*.

Transition Level: The level that links the *astral* and *light planes*, through which most souls progress relatively swiftly after death while experiencing *delayering*. However some souls can remain trapped in an aspect of this level referred to as the *grey place*.

Trapped Soul Energies/Spirits: Spirits who, after death, fail to recognize that they are dead, or remain so attached to the physical plane that they remain unaware of the existence and pull of the *light realms*. They remain trapped in the *astral plane*, and can form an *attachment* to an incarnate person, place or object.

Triggers: Emotional or even physical reminders implanted in the *light realms* for the incarnate person to recognize that there is an *emotional lesson* to be worked on, or a choice to be made that is relevant to their *life path*.

Unresolved Emotions: Strong emotions from earthly experience, usually with negative connotations – such as feelings of loss, guilt, failure, shame, remorse, selfishness, sorrow, humiliation, jealousy, anger, hatred or revenge – that are not fully dealt with or assimilated during the interlife, and therefore unintentionally carried over into the next incarnation as part of a *reactive pattern*.

Veil of Amnesia: The process by which a reincarnating soul gradually loses their memory of the *light realms* and of their *life planning* and *path*. The aim is twofold, both to prevent homesickness and so that we are not 'taking an exam knowing all the answers in advance'. The imposition of the veil is partly related to the *relayering* process, although it is not completed until early childhood. The extent of veiling may be related to the proportion of soul energy brought into incarnation, and may also be the subject of deliberate experimentation from the *light realms*.

Vibration Aspects: The different facets of the *Guide/Group Level* of the *light realms*, which are inhabited by different *soul groups* and *spirit guides* based on their level of experience. The higher this is, the higher

165

the energy vibration.

Walk-Ins: The idea that a soul can vacate an adult human body to allow another soul to walk in.

Wise Ones: Another term used for *elders*, although it can also mean souls who operate at even *higher levels*.

SOURCE REFERENCES

See the bibliography for further book details. Note that in most cases the primary sources have not been provided, but that they can be traced via the relevant endnotes in either *The Book of the Soul* of *Genesis Unveiled*. The other references are for a few more specific points of detail.

INTRODUCTION

Lawton, *The Book of the Soul*: detailed evidence and analysis of children who remember past lives, chapter 3; detailed evidence and analysis of past-life regression research, chapter 4, pp. 62–85; detailed history of interlife research, chapter 4, pp. 85–9; detailed analysis of reliability of interlife material, chapter 4, pp. 90–2; detailed summary and analysis of the pioneering interlife research, chapters 5 and 6; detailed analysis of the dynamics of karma, chapter 7.

Tomlinson, *Exploring the Eternal Soul*: new analysis of the personal interlife experience.

Modi, *Memories of God and Creation*: exploration of more universal information about origins, although with a heavy Christian bias.

Cannon, *The Convoluted Universe (Books 1 and 2)*: exploration of more universal information about a variety of favorite 'alternative' topics.

CHAPTER 1: UNUSUAL SOUL BEHAVIOR

Lawton, *The Book of the Soul*: spirit attachment, chapter 9, pp. 225–33; walk-ins, chapter 9, pp. 238–40; imprints, chapter 9, pp. 241–3; children with birthmarks and defects, chapter 3, pp. 50–8; birthmarks and defects as reminders of unassimilated emotions, chapter 7, pp. 157–8 and 164; suicide, chapter 7, pp. 173–4; regression evidence against the notion of hell and its political motivation in various religions, chapter 7, pp. 182–97; demonic possession, chapter 9, pp. 234–5.

CHAPTER 2: SOUL DEVELOPMENT

Lawton, *The Book of the Soul*: Krishna on non-asceticism, chapter 7, pp. 191; lack of dichotomy between soul unity and individuality, chapter 9, pp. 240–1 (expanded on in *Bridging the Great Divide*, a paper at www.rspress.org/se3.htm); collective nature of animal soul energy, the Introduction0, pp. 250–2; levels in astral and light planes, the Introduction0, pp. 257–9; repetitive and progressive soul behavior and blank interlife experiences, chapter 7, pp. 154–76; incarnation on and experience of other planets, the Introduction0, pp. 263–5.

Newton, *Destiny of Souls*: creation of new souls, chapter 5, pp. 125–33;

167

reshaping or remodeling of traumatized souls, chapter 4, pp. 94–104; specialist training, chapter 8, pp. 323–54.

Lawton, *Genesis Unveiled*: Hindu universal cycles, chapter 6, pp. 120–3; origin myths and dawn of Brahma, the Introduction6; monadic cycles of solar logos, the Introduction8 (this is a summary of Fortune's *The Cosmic Doctrine*).

CHAPTER 3: HUMANITY'S PAST AND FUTURE

Lawton, *Genesis Unveiled*: emergence of *Homo sapiens*, the Introduction0, p. 178; earliest evidence of deliberate burial, the Introduction0, pp. 183 and 188–9; anomalous artifacts, the Introduction1; critique of the Hindu Creationists, chapter 9, pp. 164–8 (expanded on in *Problems With Anomalous Human Remains*, a paper at www.ianlawton.com/ahr1.htm); key dates in the Pleistocene epoch, the Introduction2, pp. 206–7; Upper Paleolithic explosion, the Introduction0, pp. 183–5; impetuous fallen angels, chapter 3, pp. 63–4; creation of man traditions, chapter 8; more on pre-human soul experiments, epilogue, pp. 383–4; theosophical and other Atlantean/Lemurian material, chapters 13 and 14; earliest Neolithic settlements, the Introduction0, pp. 186–7; Atlantis as soul memory of another planet, epilogue, p. 384; common origin traditions, the Introduction6; evidence for major catastrophe in late Pleistocene, the Introduction2; golden age of spirituality, chapter 5.

Lawton, *The Book of the Soul*: pre-human soul experiments, the Introduction0, pp. 268–9; idea of human-type blueprint, the Introduction0, pp. 265–7; automatic level of amnesia, the Introduction0, pp. 272–3; soul logistics of population increase, the Introduction0, pp. 250–4 and 264–5; ethereal pressure for reduction in levels of amnesia, the Introduction0, pp. 269–70.

Newton, *Journey of Souls*: pre-human soul experiments, the Introduction1, p. 171; ethereal pressure for reduction in levels of amnesia, conclusion, p. 276.

Newton, *Destiny of Souls*: designer souls, chapter 8, pp. 334–44; Atlantis as soul memory of another planet, chapter 4, p. 100; hybrid souls, chapter 4, p. 100.

CHAPTER 4: REALITY AND TIME

Lawton, *Quantum Theory: Spiritual Panacea or Red Herring?* (paper at www.rspress.org/se5.htm): fuller discussion of the interactions between quantum theory and a spiritual worldview.

Lawton, *Reality and Time* (paper at www.rspress.org/se2.htm): idea of collectively created physical reality, and discussion of possible feedback loops.

Lawton, *Revised Meditation Affirmations for Rational Spiritualists* (paper at www.rspress.org/ma1.htm): practical spiritual advice encapsulated in a small number of affirmations.

Lawton, *Eckhart Tolle's The Power of Now* (paper at www.rspress.org/se4.htm): summary of the important ideas in Tolle's book and how they can be integrated into a Rational Spiritual worldview.

Hagelin et al, 'Effects of group practice of the Transcendental Meditation program on preventing violent crime in Washington DC', *Social Indicators Research* Vol 47 No 2 (1999), pp. 153–201 (see also www.istpp.org/crime_prevention/index.html and www.permanentpeace.org).

www.en.wikipedia.org/wiki/time_travel: thorough explanation of why time travel in the physical plane has yet to be logically explained.

Lawton, *The Book of the Soul*: tapestry containing most probably envisaged future, chapter 8, pp. 216–22; predictions of individual future via progression, chapter 8, pp. 209–16; predictions of global future via group progressions, chapter 8, pp. 198–209.

APPENDIX 1: RESEARCH DETAILS

Tomlinson, *Healing the Eternal Soul*: the techniques used in interlife regression, chapter 7 and appendix III.

BIBLIOGRAPHY

This bibliography is strictly limited to those books I have specifically referenced in this work. The date quoted is for the imprint or edition I have personally consulted, although the original date of publication may have been earlier.

Cannon, Dolores, *Between Death and Life: Conversations With a Spirit*, Gateway, 2003.

Cannon, Dolores, *The Convoluted Universe: Books 1 and 2*, Ozark Mountain Publishers, 2001 and 2005.

Fiore, Edith, *You Have Been Here Before: A Psychologist Looks at Past Lives*, Ballantine Books, 1979.

Fiore, Edith, *The Unquiet Dead: A Psychologist Treats Spirit Possession*, Ballantine Books, 1988.

Lawton, Ian, *Genesis Unveiled: The Lost Wisdom of our Forgotten Ancestors*, Virgin, 2004.

Lawton, Ian, *The Book of the Soul: Rational Spirituality for the Twenty-First Century*, Rational Spirituality Press, 2004.

Modi, Shakuntala, *Remarkable Healings: A Psychiatrist Uncovers Unsuspected Roots of Mental and Physical Illness*, Hampton Roads, 1997.

Modi, Shakuntala, *Memories of God and Creation: Remembering from the Subconscious Mind*, Hampton Roads, 2000.

Newton, Michael, *Journey of Souls: Case Studies of Life Between Lives*, Llewellyn, 2002 (5th edition).

Newton, Michael, *Destiny of Souls: New Case Studies of Life Between Lives*, Llewellyn, 2003.

Newton, Michael, *Life Between Lives: Hypnotherapy for Spiritual Regression*, Llewellyn, 2004.

Ramster, Peter, *The Truth about Reincarnation*, Rigby, 1980.

Ramster, Peter, *The Search for Lives Past*, Somerset Film & Publishing, 1992.

Stevenson, Ian, *Where Reincarnation and Biology Intersect*, Praeger, 1997.

TenDam, Hans, *Deep Healing: A Practical Outline of Past-Life Therapy*, Tasso Publishing, 1996.

TenDam, Hans, *Exploring Reincarnation*, Rider, 2003.

Tomlinson, Andy, *Healing the Eternal Soul: Insights from Past Life and Spiritual Regression*, O Books, 2006.

Tomlinson, Andy, *Exploring the Eternal Soul: Insights from the Life Between Lives*, O Books, 2007.

Wambach, Helen, *Reliving Past Lives: The Evidence Under Hypnosis*, Hutchinson, 1979.

Wambach, Helen, *Life Before Life*, Bantam, 1979.

Weiss, Brian, *Many Lives, Many Masters*, Piatkus, 1994.

Whitton, Joel, and Fisher, Joe, *Life Between Life*, Warner Books, 1988.

Woolger, Roger, *Other Lives, Other Selves: A Jungian Psychotherapist Discovers Past Lives*, Bantam, 1988.

EXPLORING THE ETERNAL SOUL
by Andy Tomlinson
O Books, 2007
www.obooks.com

'For those sincerely interested in understanding the nature of our eternal soul this book is a revelation and an inspiration. A fascinating read!' Arthur E Roffey, former Vice President of the *Society for Spiritual Regression*

'By presenting his own research and incorporating the contribution of all the pioneers in this field, this book gives credibility to the existence of memories of the life-between-lives. A must-read for those interested in finding out more about their eternal soul and for professionals wanting to explore this area in their work with clients.' Ilja van de Griend, President of the *European Association for Regression Therapy*

'It allows the reader to gain a better sense of the soul not only through Andy's own studies but through a variety of pioneers as well.' Michael Newton, author of *Journey of Souls* and *Destiny of Souls.*

Find out more about what happens after death. Follow the fascinating journey of a group of ordinary people who have been regressed though a past life and into the afterlife. Using deep hypnosis the most amazing soul memories surface of the spirit world that awaits us all. Piece by piece the book uncovers each step of the journey and is full of illuminating case study extracts.

THE BOOK OF THE SOUL
by Ian Lawton
Rational Spirituality Press, 2004
www.rspress.org

'This fine book is masterly and scholarly.' Edith Fiore, pioneering regression therapist and author of *You Have Been Here Before*

'I will be recommending this book to my students. Intellectuals need not be ashamed of having it on their shelves.' Hans TenDam, pioneering regression therapist and author of *Exploring Reincarnation*

Rational spirituality... surely this is a contradiction in terms?

How can spirituality be rational, when it relies on faith and revelation?

The simple answer is it does not have to any more.

Modern science tells us there is far more to the universe than the physical world we all perceive. The explanation that most closely fits the facts for a range of verifiable phenomena, from near-death experiences to past-life memories, is that the soul exists separately from the physical body and reincarnates repeatedly.

This book could only have been written in the twenty-first century, because it uses the latest breakthroughs in scientific and psychological research to produce a truly revolutionary view of spirituality. By comparing this modern evidence with thousands of years of spiritual traditions, it finally provides rational answers to some of the most significant and intriguing questions ever posed:

- What experiences do we have in the interlife between incarnations?

- Do we plan all the major circumstances of our lives, both good and bad?

- Does karma really involve 'action and reaction', or a far more subtle dynamic of learning, experience and growth?

Piece by piece, this book uncovers startling evidence to support a scientific and rational belief in reincarnation and the interlife. It brings together a wide range of research – including the incredible insights of thousands of ordinary regression subjects – in a logical, objective way to produce a major breakthrough in our approach to spirituality. The spiritual worldview it describes is coherent and rational, and has the capability to propel humanity forwards to previously unexplored levels... if only we will let it.